REAL MONEY ANSWERS®
FOR
COLLEGE LIFE AND BEYOND

By

PERSONAL FINANCE AUTHOR, SPEAKER, COACH & BLOGGER

PATRICE C. WASHINGTON

Seek Wisdom Find Wealth

Atlanta Los Angeles

Real Money Answers for College Life and Beyond

www.seekwisdomfindwealth.com

ISBN # 978-0-615-57598-8

Published by Seek Wisdom Find Wealth, Mableton, GA 30126

Printed in the United States of America

First Printing, April 2012

Photography by Chad Finley

Cover Design by Petie Parker

This book is available at quantity discounts for bulk purchases. For information, please call (404) 913-4479.

To my family for your unwavering
support, love and encouragement.

You are the purest example of
God's unconditional love for me.

And, to that guy who signed me up for
my first credit card in college,

I have no idea where that t-shirt and Frisbee are,

but thanks for the life lessons.

Today I share them with the world.

CONTENTS

INTRODUCTION

PERSONAL FINANCE. A topic rarely discussed at the dinner table and if you're like many, probably avoided by your parents almost as often as sex. Like sex, whether it's discussed or not the chances that you will engage in either are very high and can be detrimental if simple principles are not learned early on.

I know where you may be right now if you're a college kid already up to your eyeballs in credit card debt OR you're the total opposite; petrified to engage in even the most basic financial matters for a fear of ending up like so and so. Either way, I was there too! After being scared to even look at a credit card much less swipe one, ironically, I managed to leave college with almost $18k of credit card debt. I received tons of grants, scholarships, school loans, parental assistance and even worked a full-time job my entire collegiate career. I never had to put a textbook on credit. I never needed a cash advance to cover rent like many of my friends. There were no designer purses to show for the debt or even a lavish spring break trip to reminisce upon. Making one small poor decision after another in less than four years led me to a massive $18,000 worth of debt!

The little I did hear about personal finance I attempted to incorporate every once in a while. The problem is that typically what I heard came from a fellow student who was just as misguided as I was. It's not like I was dumb; far from it actually. After making the Dean's List several times at a prestigious university, I can honestly say that academically I was stellar, but, eh, financially, I was well . . . just plain ignorant!

Why should this matter to you? Because, oftentimes smart college kids are typically the ones who make a complete wreck out of their financial lives because of making small, misguided and completely avoidable decisions. Don't be fooled! Smart people do dumb things all the time . . . especially in the area of finance. I know that oftentimes people believe they are wise because of a school or university they have attended or degrees they have earned. It is true that seeking higher education will provide you with knowledge, but it is important not to confuse the two. Knowledge is basically having the facts. But, wisdom is applying those facts to real life. It means nothing to merely know something without knowing when, how and where to use it. Taking into consideration that this principle is especially true in the area of personal finance, don't beat yourself up about where you are. Your present location has nothing to do with your future destination.

If you learn nothing else, know that time is on your side. I paid that $18,000 debt off in less than 24 months and turned my life around and so can you! Understanding anything about personal finance will make you so much more competitive and successful as you enter the real world. As a real estate and mortgage broker, I had clients well into their 30s, 40s and 50s who were clueless about a few of the simple, yet fundamental concepts you will read over the next several pages. Please know that you are so far ahead of the game right now and this book is just the first step in making sure you play to win!

This journey is going to be a process that will take hard work and effort on your part. Being sound financially is a personal choice, hence the term *personal finance.* By implementing the lessons you learn here, as well as continuing to seek out answers to your most pressing money questions, you will establish your dedication toward defining and determining your own destiny. Will this guide answer all the financial questions you'll ever have? Absolutely not! At least I hope you don't stop here; my goal is to introduce you to the basic financial knowledge that many who have come before you, educated or not, have managed to elude and thus elude the success they were called to. This is just a start! But believe me, my true goal is to leave you thirsting for more; answering many questions, but leaving you with a desire to learn more and more.

Remember to never become complacent as many have, concluding that academic courses will provide all the keys to financial success's door. Do the work now and your future payoff will be greater than you can even imagine today. . . I promise. ☺

HOW TO USE THIS BOOK

There are two ways to read the *Real Money Answers* series. Although it's written in a question and answer format, it can be read like any other book, straight through from beginning to end. It is divided into ten parts that build on each other in natural progression. Reading it in order will give you a solid understanding of the personal finance issues most prevalent for young adults and college students getting their first taste of adult financial responsibility.

On the other hand, this book was written to be a resource guide for you to refer to for years to come. It's written in subject specific sections to help you quickly get your questions answered. Because it's such an easy read, however, if you have any questions about a particular topic, you may as well read the entire section until you begin to commit the information to memory. As you will soon learn, results are based on actions, actions on thoughts, thoughts on beliefs and beliefs are formed by the information you allow into your mind. In order for you to achieve the intended result, financial independence, you will have to actually apply the answers you read on these pages.

Remember knowledge is nothing without application. The principles that lie within these pages will only be beneficial when you put them into practice. In order to help you jumpstart the implementation, I suggest you keep a special notebook or three-ring binder to keep your notes in. Personally, I dedicate a journal each year to my professional, personal and financial development. As you encounter personal reflection assignments or other concepts which strike a chord for you, record your thoughts there.

This will show you how much you have learned and accomplished in any given period of time. You can't do it all in one day, but progress beats perfection any day. Enjoy.

LOOK FOR THESE HELPFUL NOTES THROUGHOUT

Quotes and expressions to remember

Savings tips or financial illustrations

Statistics or stories that need to stick

FIRST THINGS FIRST: GET YOUR MIND RIGHT

THIS BOOK WAS CREATED to give you quick, simple and real answers to some of your most pressing money questions. Though I knew you would ask obvious questions about credit cards and student loans, I also knew that I had to give you the answers to questions you may not even think to ask at this stage in your journey. First Things First is about giving you what I consider to be the foundation of personal finance success. It's about teaching you the basic principle that any successful person will share with you: True success starts on the inside; the outside is just the byproduct. Too often people assume that if they just learned how to write out a budget or balance a checkbook all of their financial worries would magically disappear. They fail to realize, however, that the desire and discipline to do both consistently must come from somewhere else; it starts with your thoughts, beliefs and most importantly your mindset toward money.

The back of my business cards read *"Changing roots, changing fruits, changing lives . . ."* When I hand them out, I always get asked to explain what I mean by that tagline. In a nutshell, fruits represent the results we see in our lives each day. Your bank account balance, where you live, the opportunities that come your way, the relationships you currently have are all of your fruits or outcomes. When people desire to make a change in these areas, they falsely assume that if they switch banks or move to a new city or dump the person they're dating, that everything in their lives will become better. But what happens when the same results creep back up even in a new environment or with a new person? Quite frankly, you end up with the same fruits! Until you change your roots, the stuff deep down on the inside that causes you to think or act a certain way, you will never change your fruits and subsequently, you will never change your life.

What you view as success from any angle was usually preceded by a combination of hard work on both the inside and outside. The personal finance aspect of life is no different. Contrary to popular belief, financial success isn't really about money at all; it's about creating a supportive mind-set toward money. So, get ready to learn the stuff you didn't even know you needed to know. First things first!

WHAT IS PERSONAL FINANCE?

Personal finance deals with your individual relationship with money. It serves as your financial blueprint; speaking to the way you obtain, budget, save, spend and manage monetary resources overall. These behaviors are assessed at various stages throughout your lifetime, taking into account a mixture of financial risks, as well as major life events like getting your first job or getting married.

Some of the major components of personal finance may include checking and savings accounts, credit cards, consumer and student loans, investment principles, income tax management and much more depending on which phase of life you are in. Despite which stage you fall into at any given time in your life, a positive relationship with money forces you to continuously assess the questions: "How much money and financial assets do I possess today?", "How much money will I need at various points in the future?" and "How do I go about getting that money in the present?"

These questions are the foundation for creating a personal financial plan. The most basic plan will always include these five steps:

1. Assessment: *Where are you now?*

2. Goal Setting: *Where do you want to be?*

3. Creating a Plan: *How will you get there?*

4. Execution: *Taking action and making it happen.*

5. Re-Assessment: *Repeating the process regularly.*

At some point in this section, I suggest visiting Appendix C – Assorted Worksheets and completing your very own personal financial plan! (Hint: This is where a notebook or journal for personal development would come in handy.)

WHAT IS THE MOST IMPORTANT FINANCIAL PRINCIPLE I SHOULD KNOW?

The most important financial principle to remember is that to achieve success in your finances and any other area of life, your mindset toward wealth creation must be on the correct setting. Your thoughts, actions and feelings toward money must be shaped on the inside before positive results manifest on the outside.

As I often say, your roots create your fruits. No matter how much money you accumulate in your life, if you're not ready to receive it on the inside, you're outside will never allow you to keep it. Being financially sound takes having a mindset that you are determined to seek out those opportunities to learn more about what you know you don't know, as well as those things you have no idea you don't know.

Becoming wealthy has 100% nothing to do with money and 100% everything to do with YOU and your mindset towards money.

Some time ago, I heard a wonderful New Year's sermon in which the pastor asserted that it was extremely important to realize how important who you need to be is in relationship to setting goals for where you want to go and what you want to have. The pastor shared that many people have gifts and talents that will take them to celebrated places in life where their characters could never maintain nor sustain them. Is that deep or what? Think about the entertainers, athletes and other celebrated figures in society who have amassed great fortunes only to end up on the E network's "True Hollywood Story" explaining how they lost it all. Don't shake your head or point your finger. You are no different! If you don't begin digging deep and strengthening your roots now, tomorrow's fruits will never change and the life you desire may be attainable, but will never remain sustainable.

If you plan on being successful on this very often sacrificial journey, then you must make up in your mind right now that where you want to go and who you want to be outweighs what anyone else thinks about you. Decide now that you will maintain a "whatever it takes" attitude. Resolve that you will not place a lot of weight on what anyone else thinks of your plan. Understand that this journey takes refusing to be "normal" and live paycheck to paycheck like most Americans. Decide today that you will take control of your mindset in order to take control of your life. *Are you ready?*

MY PARENTS DIDN'T TEACH ME ANYTHING ABOUT MONEY... WHAT SHOULD I DO?

Get over it! I know this probably seems like a cruel answer, but the bottom line is everyone has something they can legitimately blame their parents for doing or not doing that has negatively impacted their life. At some point, however, you have to be an adult and let it go if you are truly to move on with your own life.

If your parent's didn't teach you anything about money, but you're a young adult and already picking up a book like this, then you're still on the right path and you've got nothing but time to correct the wrongs of your childhood! The best thing about childhood is that it's over!

"Personal finance is 80 percent behavior and only 20 percent head knowledge."
-Dave Ramsey

Remember, your parents are someone's children too. They may have learned their habits from your beloved Gram and Pops. (See "What Determines My Financial Blueprint?") Just be happy you have a chance to break that generational cycle. All you can do now is make sure you do your part to expose your future family to a totally different mindset and blueprint towards money and wealth building principles.

WHAT DETERMINES MY FINANCIAL BLUEPRINT?

For most of us, our financial blueprint was handed down to us by our parents almost like a strand of DNA. It's important, however, to remember that no one is born with a particular attitude toward money. You were taught, just like we all were, how to act and think about money matters. These subconscious beliefs, ideals, thoughts and actions are what create your financial blueprint.

In addition to your parents, this could include siblings, friends, teachers and religious doctrine or leaders you were exposed to, to name a few. Nevertheless, no matter what age you are in life, unless first recognized and then reconditioned, it is very likely that the lessons and habits you learned as a child may have conditioned you to subconsciously sabotage your own success with money.

When determining your financial blueprint, here are a few things to consider:

Verbal Influences: What did you hear about money, wealth and rich people when you were growing up? Did anyone ever say things like *filthy rich, money can't buy love, the poor will be close to God, money is the root of all evil, it takes money to make money, or you only need enough to get by?*

____

____

____

____

Modeling: What did you witness in regards to how your parents obtained, managed and allocated money? Did they have any systems or budgets in place? Was money a source of joy for your family or did your parents argue about money often?

____

____

____

____

Specific Incidents: What experiences do you remember about money, wealth and rich people? Were you embarrassed at a cash register when a credit card was declined? Did you experience eviction notices or utility services being interrupted?

____

____

____

____

After taking a moment to record your initial thoughts, give yourself additional time to truly consider each one of these categories and complete the following exercise for each influence.

Awareness: Reflect upon the things that were said, the "ways of being" you witnessed and a specific incident you experienced in regards to money and wealth. Write down how your life today may be identical or opposite to each of them.

____

____

____

____

Understanding: Write down the effect these words, habits and incidents have had on your financial life.

____

____

____

____

Disassociation: Separate who you are today from what you saw as a child. That life was what your parents chose and you have a choice in the present moment to be different.

HOW DO I DEVELOP WEALTHY WAYS OF THINKING?

A part of being wealthy is having the mindset that money is an important tool that when utilized properly, can assist you in creating the life you want. The difference between poor people and wealthy people is simply the way they think about money. Remember, you may have grown up hearing, seeing and forming a lot of negative habits surrounding money and wealth creation. (See "What is My Financial Blueprint?") The only way to progress and move past your past is to replace your previous thinking with a new and fresh perspective. I believe in using positive affirmations to do so. Below are a few samples of what I used to change my thinking! Create your own in the spaces provided and recite them daily.

Old Way of Thinking:	**"I'm clueless about money. I don't even know where to start."**
New Way of Thinking:	**"I am ready, willing and able to manage my money!"**
Old Way of Thinking:	**"It's just a penny. That's nothing."**
New Way of Thinking:	**"The cents matter just as much as the dollars do! I love ALL money!"**
Old Way of Thinking:	**"Money is hard to come by."**
New Way of Thinking:	**"Money flows to me easily, freely and often!"**
Old Way of Thinking:	**"Rich people have all the luck."**
New Way of Thinking:	**"Profitable opportunities always come my way!"**
Old Way of Thinking:	"______________________________"
New Way of Thinking:	"______________________________"
Old Way of Thinking:	"______________________________"
New Way of Thinking:	"______________________________"

WHAT CAN I DO TO CREATE WEALTHY HABITS?

This is a question students ask often. However, once I provide the points below, I always wonder by their bulging eyes or scant notes, whether they will ever do them. Most people understand the saying that we are creatures of habit. The part they don't get, however, is that when you don't do anything to change negative habits, then you are already in the habit of not doing. I often tell the young people I meet to stop telling me what they are *trying* to do. You're either doing or you're not doing. You either have doing habits or not-doing habits. Reading is one thing, but being in the habit of doing something is what creates success. The choice is yours.

DEFINE YOUR GOALS

It's impossible to get *what* you want if you aren't exactly sure of what you want. You need to be clear about your intentions in order to bring them forth. You must write them down and be as concise with any details, as possible – especially those dealing with numbers or financial objectives. You'll be amazed at how opportunities come about and begin to lead you in the direction of your goal.

Ex. I will save $750 from my summer internship.

DECLARE A PURPOSE

You have to know the "why" behind what you want. Without declaring a purpose, you'll continue to live in the moment and blindly throw money away. Knowing the "why" of what you are doing, will keep you focused on reaching both long- and short-term goals.

"Having more money would allow me to . . ."
Ex. . . . graduate from college with minimal debt.
Ex. . . . treat myself to a dream graduation trip.

UNDERSTAND YOUR VALUE

Understanding your value allows you to create wealth by knowing what to charge for your service or product. (See "How Do I Create Cash in College?") We are all blessed with unique abilities and talents. Selling ourselves short is an insult to God. He gives us the ability to produce wealth, but when we don't maximize that potential to the fullest, we can't turn around and beg God for much more else financially. Once you understand and declare your value, you will be much more confident in charging what you are worth and communicating that to potential clientele.

Ex. Sharing my knowledge of social networking with small-business owners surrounding my campus allows them to maximize their marketing dollars and achieve their goals.

SEE AND BELIEVE

It is so vital to create a visual representation of your goals. I have always used picture journals and dream boards as a focal point in turning imagination into reality. Find magazine photos or pictures online and post them somewhere where you can see them at least daily. Use the power of your visual sense to keep you focused on your goal. This focus is what will keep you motivated over the long term.

REMAIN GRATEFUL

When you remain grateful, you allow yourself to find wealth in whatever situation you may be experiencing at any given moment. When you are grateful for what you already have as well as those things you desire, you become happier and healthier and continue to attract more of the same.

DEVELOP A "SO WHAT, NOW WHAT" ATTITUDE

The reality is that obstacles are going to be thrown your way no matter how much positive thinking and prayer you use. Instead of allowing life's distractions to throw you off course, you have to accept them, learn the lesson and move on – continuously pressing toward your goals. When you can look life head on and say, "XYZ challenge has occurred, but what can I do now to move on?" you will reach goals you never thought were possible! Taking on this type of attitude teaches you to act in spite of your own doubts, ridicule from others, fears, etc. When you press on despite the unexpected, you build courage and take down challenges one by one!

GIVE WELL, RECEIVE WELL

Believe it or not, many of us are neither good at giving nor receiving. You may think you are, but if you really studied your answers to everyday things like people giving you a compliment or you having the ability to do something nice for an absolute stranger, you'd be shocked at what you would discover.

The bottom line is giving and receiving work in perfect harmony. You must give, in order to receive and the more you receive, the more you are expected to give again. Have you noticed how philanthropic the world's wealthiest people are? As much as you've heard about their giving, you don't see Oprah or Bill Gates running out of money!

WHY SHOULD I CARE ABOUT WHAT'S GOING ON IN THE ECONOMY?

Many people believe and live as if the economy's trials or triumphs are independent of the financial economy within their own homes. Unfortunately, this simply isn't true. You must stay aware of what goes on in the real world because this actually does have a huge impact on your personal life. This is not to say that if the national economy is in a slump, you will have to be, but it may affect job opportunities that you are banking on or how your investments perform.

One of the beauties of being financially sound is being able to weather the ups and downs of the national economy. Being prepared to mitigate financial woes in the economy is a huge benefit to planning, saving and investing. Unlike a staggering number of Americans, you'll be able to withstand the storm because you already live beneath your means, debt-free and with plenty of money in savings to support yourself should you encounter job loss or any other financially devastating occurrence.

12.8 million young people under the age of 30 are either unemployed, working part-time or working at a job that doesn't require a college degree.

- Andrew Sum, economist at Northeastern University citing data from U.S. Bureau of Labor Statistics

I started my first business at 21 years old when the real estate market was booming. Economists had long forewarned that the housing bubble may burst, but the money kept rolling in and being young and naïve, I refused to take heed to economists' reports. When it was all said and done, the bubble did burst and a lot of us in the industry were left soaking wet! I wish I would've gotten out earlier, but at least I had savings for that very rainy season!

WHAT RESOURCES SHOULD I USE TO KEEP UP WITH WHAT'S GOING ON IN FINANCE AND THE ECONOMY?

I wholeheartedly suggest reading material from a diverse group of personal finance authors and bloggers until you find a method and style of planning, saving or investing that works with you, for you and coincides with your values. There's no one way to do anything in life. The goal is just that you take action and do something! I've been reading about this stuff for years and there's no one interpretation that I can honestly say I agree with 100 percent. Take what works for you and feel free to leave behind the parts that don't.

A few of my blog recommendations are listed here because I know how quickly we all want our information these days, but there is a complete list in Appendix A – Print Resources.

BOOKS WORTH READING:

Secrets of the Millionaire Mind	T. Harv Eker
The Magic of Thinking Big	David Schwartz
Live It Love It Earn It	Marianna Olszewski
Young, Fabulous & Broke	Suze Orman
You're So Money	Farnoosh Tarobi

BLOGS TO SUBSCRIBE TO:

www.seekwisdomfindwealth.com (of, course a shameless plug!)
www.budgetsaresexy.com
www.genxfinance.com
www.moneyunder30.com
www.thesimpledollar.com
www.youngadultfinances.com
www.mintlife.com
www.studenomics.com
www.singleguymoney.com
www.20somethingfinance.com

BEATING BANKRUPTCY: THE KEY TO BUDGETING & ORGANIZING

DO YOU THINK YOU ARE too young to worry about bankruptcy? Think again. Research shows that in the last 10 years, bankruptcy filings by 18-25 year olds have increased some 96 percent. As a matter of fact, studies have found that in 2001, 2002 and 2006, more young people filed for bankruptcy than graduated from college. If you take a look around your classroom right now, some poor unsuspecting student will be filing for bankruptcy less than two years after they earn their degree, assuming they even do that. Now, let's just hope we're not talking about you! I can guarantee you that most people who file bankruptcy do not stick to a sound plan which truly reflects and supports their lifestyle. Additionally, they are unaware of what their financial situation looks like until they are overwhelmed by debt and their back is up against the wall. The key to beating bankruptcy is creating and sticking to a believable budget and staying organized.

WHAT IS BANKRUPTCY IN SIMPLE TERMS?

In simple terms, bankruptcy is the legal process that allows individuals or businesses who are stuck in a financial crisis to settle their debts under a bankruptcy court's protection. Although the term is used often and seemingly easily defined, the long-term implications, emotional scars and embarrassment it carries are much more difficult to put into words.

TWO MOST COMMON TYPES OF BANKRUPTCY:

1. **Chapter 7 Bankruptcy** - Chapter 7 bankruptcy is known as "straight bankruptcy" and is the preferred option for people with little or no property and a lot of unsecured debt. It is a liquidation bankruptcy meaning that the court will sell any non-exempt assets you have to pay your creditors and regardless of the amount paid, discharge that debt.

   Since October 2005, there is a "means test" applied to applicants for Chapter 7 Bankruptcy. You must be earning less than the average income of your state (check www.usdoj.gov/ust). If you are above your state's median, then you can still file for Chapter 7 if your excess income cannot pay your debts over 5 years AND cannot pay 25 percent of your unsecured debt over that period.

   Chapter 7 bankruptcy does not discharge all debts. Student loans remain, as well as previous judgments on alimony and child support. State or federal tax bills must still be paid, as well. If you keep your home or car, all payments on these must be kept up.

2. **Chapter 13 Bankruptcy** - Chapter 13 Bankruptcy, sometimes called the wage earner's plan, or reorganization bankruptcy, is quite different from Chapter 7 bankruptcy (which wipes out most of your debts). In a Chapter 13 bankruptcy, you use your income to pay some or all of what you owe to your creditors over time - anywhere from three to five years, depending on the size of your debts and income.

   You must have a regular income and owe less than $250,000.00 in unsecured debt and $750,000.00 in secured debt. These debts must also be non-contingent and liquidated, meaning that they must be for a certain, fixed amount and not subject to any conditions.

! UN REAL

In the last 10 years, bankruptcy filings by 18-25 year olds have increased some 96 percent.

Always remember that despite the "fresh start" you hear about bankruptcy providing, there are definitely long-term implications. Chapter 7 bankruptcies remain on your credit history for 10 years after the event and Chapter

13 bankruptcies will stay on your history for seven years after you file. In addition, either filing will drop your FICO score a minimum of 100 points and an average of 250 points.

CAN YOU DEFINE A "NEED" VS. A "WANT"?

This is one of the most important questions in personal finance, which is why it's also one of the most overlooked. The false perception is that the concept is so simple and everyone should just know. The reality, however, is that while many can define the words "need" and "want", it is difficult for most people to assess them during the most important time: when they're at the mall making impulse buys or even when they set out to create a budget.

What have you heard? That a need is clothing, food and shelter? And, let me guess, that a want is *everything* else? Well that type of answer goes back to the verbal influences we learned about earlier. (See "What Determines My Financial Blueprint?")

Because needs and wants are different for different people and may even change for the same person at a different stage in their life, it's impossible to provide a specific and clear cut list of needs and wants.

I define a "need" as something that is *absolutely* necessary to your well being. Does that include clothing, food, and shelter? Absolutely! But it may also include a cell phone or Internet connection or gas depending on what the necessities are for you being able to support yourself.

In addition, my definition of a "want" is something that you would prefer to have and you perceive will make a beneficial impact on your life rather than a bad. Although we can all make great cases for the "extras" in life, wants become detrimental to your financial success when their purchase is impulsive and not planned and saved for within your budget.

To that matter, I also don't believe that a person, who cannot consistently handle their necessities, should bother with any extras unless it is to reward them for making great strides in their financial planning. And by great strides I mean actually reaching measurable, achievable and supportive goals. I don't mean "I saved $100 and now I can spend $80 on jeans or video games."

Needs and wants are different for different people and may even change for the same person at a different stage in their life.

HOW DO I MAKE A BUDGET?

A personal budget is a finance plan that allocates future personal income toward expenses, savings and debt repayment. The idea of a budget is actually quite simple, despite it becoming a taboo term in a culture that moronically believes you should have what you want, when you want it, and worry about the consequences in bankruptcy court.

To create a budget, you must look at your past spending, as well as future income. There are several methods and tools available for creating, using and adjusting a personal budget. Although I've listed the most basic categories for you to include in your budget, I honestly don't care what version you use as long as you use one. Just remember that keeping it simple will keep it achievable. There's no reason for a college student to use the same budget their parents use. Only keep the parts that work for you and toss out anything that has nothing to do with your life at this stage. The simpler your budget, the better. Or, as my high school teacher, Mr. Buckner, would say, "Keep things simple stupid and everything will be fine."

Try online budgeting sites like mint.com or mvelopes.com. You can track spending and financial goals all in one place.

STUFF TO INCLUDE IN YOUR BUDGET:

Income
Earned Income (Money You Worked For)
Financial Aid
Support from Parents

Expenses
Charitable Giving
Savings
Rent
Utilities
Cell Phone
Car Insurance
Groceries
Fuel
Books & School Supplies
Cable (No, it's not a utility!)

See Appendix C for a sample budget.

HOW CAN I BUDGET INCONSISTENT INCOME?

Budgeting an irregular income is going to be a tad bit trickier, but it's not an impossible task. The two things you must always keep in mind are that although your income may vary greatly, many of your expenses will not. So even if you have a great month, you have to plan ahead and recognize that at some point in the future you could run into a not so great month. You also have to keep in mind that you may not know the exact dates for when your income actually comes in and since you don't get to choose when your accidents or emergencies come up, you may very well have a need for extra money before even your basic needs are taken care of or your average income has been met.

Use the steps below to help you with budgeting inconsistent income.

1. **Determine your average monthly income.** The more months you can include, the better, but don't use any less than three months to determine your average. If you've had a substantial windfall that is out of the ordinary or some other income that you know is not reoccurring, then don't include it at all. This is your time to create a realistic plan for your life moving forward. Utilizing any misleading information from the past will only hurt your future planning.

2. **Decrease non-necessities.** Once you figure out your monthly average income, compare it with your monthly expenses. If your expenditures can ONLY be met on your "good months" then you have some cutting out to do. Your expenses must be based on your average monthly income; NOT the great months which can come few and maybe even far in between. Anything that is putting you over budget and can be labelled a "want" should be put aside until you can increase your income for at least 3 months consecutively.

3. **Declare a cushion.** To plan for the unexpected events, I suggest creating a cushion within your budget of about five percent or 10 percent. In essence, I'm asking that you not budget to the last penny. Every unexpected event that occurs doesn't have to be a state of emergency. What if you are out on a sweltering day and really need a nice cold bottle of water? I'd hate for $0.99 to break the bank!

4. **Determine a dollar amount for your opportunity fund.** No matter how inconsistent your income is, one thing is certain; you must pay yourself before you pay anyone else if you plan on truly becoming wealthy. Many leading financial writers may call this an "emergency fund," however, I just cannot bring myself to use those words. I believe that what you verbalize, you magnify in your life. So, if you wait for a rainy day, then you get a hurricane. Instead, allow your "opportunity fund" the ability to take care of any possibilities, good or not so good that may come your way. This will help you on the months when your earning is below the average.

I'VE MADE A BUDGET, BUT HOW DO I STICK TO IT?

Making a budget is a marvelous first step, but far too often that's where the story ends for most people. The reason so many people give up on using a budget is because the one they have created is far too rigid, intimidating, complicated and restrictive. In order to create a budget you can stick to, I suggest that you recognize the following:

1. **Attitude** – First and foremost, your attitude toward creating a budget has to be healthy. If you think that budgets stink, then guess what? . . . Your budgeting experience is going to stink! I usually have clients call their budgets something along the lines of a "Prosperity Plan" or "Wealth Building Map." The title doesn't matter as long as it gets you excited about managing and mastering your money!
2. **Purpose** - A budget should have a defined goal you would like to achieve within a specified time period. Having a goal in mind will help you keep focused when your discipline begins to feel like deprivation. Once utilizing your budget helps you obtain a goal, set another one. Never become complacent when there is always a goal you can be striving toward.
3. **Simplicity** - The more complicated you make the budgeting process, the less likely you will be willing to stick with it. At this stage in your life, a budget really does not need to be too intense.

You have to know the *why* behind what you want. Without the why, you'll never do the what and how will never matter!

(See "How do I make a budget?") More than likely you have minimal sources of income and hopefully minimal monthly expenses. Just list what directly deals with your situation and eliminate any additional fluff.

4. **Flexibility** - The budgeting process is designed to be flexible. You should recognize up front that your budget will change from month to month, and will require monthly review. For example, if you go over in one category, then it should be accounted for next month or greater efforts should be made to prevent it. Remember if you must increase in an area, then some other area must decrease. At no time can you have more going out then coming in. If you want to spend more, just figure out a way to earn more. Don't get frustrated; its basic math.

HOW CAN I KEEP FINANCES ORGANIZED?

I am a proponent of utilizing any system that is easy for you to maintain and is actually a real system and not just a shoebox under your bed. De-cluttering and organizing financial records is actually my favorite exercise to do when I'm coaching or consulting people on personal finance. Think about it: How can you have your financial life in order when your financial documents are out of order?

So let's just hop to it and get "IT" together! Getting "IT" together means that this will be your time to gather all of your important stuff in one place and put it into a system that will work for you and not against you. So wherever your "IT" is – go and get it! Pull it out of shoeboxes, off your kitchen counter, out of junk drawers, envelopes with the little months on it, or wherever you've been cramming all the bills, check stubs and other "stuff" that you swore you would organize one day. Go get "IT" because that day has arrived!

If you don't enjoy homework right now, get over it because this is one lesson you actually do need to take with you into the real world! If you learn nothing else from me, please at least incorporate this system or something pretty similar into your life. You'll thank me some day.*

You can't have your financial life in order when your financial documents are out of order.

WHAT'S NEEDED:

1 Dozen Hanging File Folders
1 Box of 25 File Folders
1 Plastic File Tote

WHAT TO DO:

STEP ONE:
Label the first hanging file folder **"Tax Returns."** In it, place three file folders, one for last year, the present year and next year. Mark the year on each folder's tab and put into it all of that year's important tax documents, like W-2 forms or 1099s. If you can't find them, but used professional tax preparers in the past, call them and ask for back copies. If you've never filed taxes, create a folder for this year because my prayer is that you would begin to earn an income by the time you finish this book . . . Okay, at least the end of the semester!

STEP TWO:
Label the second hanging folder **"Savings and Checking."** If you have several checking and savings accounts, create separate file folders for them. Keep your monthly bank statements here, as well as any ATM slips or deposit slips you retrieve during the month. (Note: If you have several accounts with no money in them, just consolidate. Don't waste time, energy or paper.)

STEP THREE:
Label the third hanging folder **"Household."** Assuming you're a renter, this should contain your lease, the receipt for your security deposit, and the receipts for your rental payments. I would also include utility folders such as "Electricity," "Gas," "Cable," etc. These are also statements you should keep up with regularly. I've caught hundreds of dollars being erroneously charged on phone and cable bills by being able to compare multiple statements over a period of time. Don't forget to also include any agreements you have between yourself and your roommates. No matter how great you are as friends, when money is involved, document everything!

STEP FOUR:
Label the fourth hanging folder **"Credit Card DEBT."** Make sure to capitalize the word DEBT so it stands out and bothers you every time you see

it. I'm not kidding! Create a separate file for each credit card account you have. (Prayerfully, this is not more than two!)

STEP FIVE:
Label the fifth hanging folder **"Loans."** Place any documents associated with your loans here. At this stage that may include student loans, car loans, personal loans, etc. Each debt should have its own file. Ex. "Sallie Mae" has one student loan folder and "Chase Student Loan" another. Each folder should contain the loan note and your statements and payment records.

STEP SIX:
Label the sixth hanging folder **"Insurance."** It will contain separate folders for each of your insurance policies, which may just be car insurance at this point, but if you have any other policies then include them here as well.

STEP SEVEN:
If you have children, put together a folder labeled **"Children's Accounts."** It should hold all statements and other records pertaining to college savings. I also added a folder for "Child Care" to keep track for tax purposes, as well as a folder with immunization records and other health-related documents.

STEP EIGHT:
Label the eighth hanging folder **"Personal."** It should contain files for personal expenses such as clothing, grooming, dental services, organization dues, etc.

As you begin the process of putting together your system, you may find you are missing some documents. Whatever the reason you have for not having them, today is a new day. That was something the old you didn't keep up with because no one taught you how much it could simplify your life. But, now that you know the truth, you can put the files together as best you can and figure out how or where to get your hands on anything that's missing. The important thing is that you've taken the first step and that is something you should definitely be proud of!

* Please note that this system has been modified for the typical college student. The full system was created by David Bach, author of Smart Couples Finish Rich.

HOW LONG SHOULD I KEEP FINANCIAL DOCUMENTS?

I know that managing your money can create a lot of paper work. Once you have your filing system in place, you can shred documents periodically to make sure you always have the most recent and relevant information. (See, "How Can I Keep My Finances Organized?") Don't drain yourself with holding on to anything longer than you have to.

If you're like me and just like to know you have something, then scan and save your documents in well organized folders on a computer, but remember to back it up often. If you opt for paperless or e-billing and receive your statements in your e-mail box, then there's no need to scan. You can simply save your statements as a PDF. Save time, paper and energy!

Here are some tips on exactly how long you should hold on to old financial records.

KEEP FOR A YEAR OR LESS:

- **Bank Statements** – Review when you receive them. Look for unauthorized purchases, and keep the last three.
- **Monthly Bills** – Review for accuracy but there's no need to keep them for more than a quarter at the most.
- **Credit Card Bills** – Review your bill for any billing errors. I suggest keeping these for at least six months.
- **Paycheck Stub** – I say you should always have your last three pay stubs. You never know when you'll need to prove income for a loan or other necessity. Keep the last few in the year to compare against your W-2 or 1099. If it doesn't match, go to your employer and request a change. Otherwise, you can shred them as your W-2 is good enough for filing taxes.
- **Insurance Policies** – Always keep the most recent policy. Old ones don't matter once a new one takes effect.

KEEP FOR 7 YEARS:

- **Tax Documents** – I know seven years seems like forever, but so will an IRS audit if you don't have your tax returns in order. You have three years to file an amended return if you think you're due a larger refund and the IRS has three years to audit you if they think you made a mistake. The IRS has six years to audit you if they think you underreported income and there is no time limit if they think you just blatantly filed a fraudulent return.

If you've lost old tax returns and would feel better if you had a copy, contact your tax preparer and if all else fails request a copy of past tax returns from the IRS. You can get a tax return transcript for free in about two weeks by calling 1-800-829-1040.

KEEP FOREVER OR INDEFINITELY:

- **Loan Documents** – Keep these for the life of the loan and destroy once you've paid it off and have title or final document proving payment in full in your possession.
- **Receipts** – Keep anything documenting a major purchase like jewelry or a computer. You never know when it can come in handy.
- **Any long-term insurance policies or investment accounts you have started should be kept until maturation.**
- **Brokerage Statements** - If you've already begun investing, you'll get monthly statements telling you how much you've made each month. Keep brokerage statements until you receive the annual statement at the end of each year. Keep annual statements until you sell the investment. You'll use them to prove your capital gains or losses when you do your taxes.

BANKING: UNDERSTANDING THE NUTS & BOLTS

TO BANK OR NOT TO BANK? This is NOT the question! There is no reason for anyone in this day and age to be uncertain of whether or not they should be "bothered" with a checking and savings account. Based on the financial DNA inherited from your parents, you very well could be the person who learned that dealing with the bank was more expensive, less convenient and less safe than dealing in a world of mattress money and money orders from the corner store. If this is true, it's not too late for you. If you grew up thinking that the ATM was somehow free money and that your parents receiving those little postcard sized notices from the bank each day was normal, it's not too late for you either. Neither scenario is ideal, but thankfully you have a chance to correct some terribly wrong patterns in your family's financial blueprint. To do so you need to understand the nuts and bolts of banking.

WHAT'S WRONG WITH USING CHECK CASHING CENTERS?

According to John Hope Bryant, founder of Operation HOPE, one of the nation's leading financial literacy organizations, "Unbanked individuals are essentially economic slaves," and I couldn't agree with him more. In order to navigate successfully through the technological era we live in today, you would be committing financial suicide if you could not enjoy the basic luxury and flexibility of your own checking account. A check cashing service refers to a company that will only do that; cash your check for a hefty fee and possibly throw in a money order for a fee as well.

An argument that I heard once while volunteering in an 8th grade classroom for Operation HOPE, was that if you don't make a lot of money, it will cost about the same to cash checks in a month as it would to pay bank fees. Another student in support of check cashing centers added that banks were "too far away and you can walk to the corner store." Look at the financial blueprint already established in such young and impressionable minds. In reality, banks obviously cash checks and in many cases at no cost to the consumer, especially one of its own customers. With direct deposit, there is generally no need for most to physically cash a check when they can have funds at their disposal to spend and pay bills via personal checks and ATM or debit cards. With the online nature of most banks, and popularity of electronic payment, the false convenience of check cashing centers gets lost when considering the ease of depositing paychecks electronically and paying bills online.

As with a bank, you still need to provide identification, and many check cashing services may not even accept personal checks. The worst part about check cashing centers is the astronomical fees. Fees from check cashing services tend to far exceed bank fees. For example, cashing a $1,000 dollar check might incur a three to five percent fee, regardless of the origin of the check. That is an average of $40 in fees for a single check! Even a 1.5 percent fee would be $15. Conversely, most banks that may charge a monthly service fee charge about $10 per month. Even this small loss of income can add up over time, and thus, ultimately prove less beneficial than the pseudo convenience of a check cashing center.

To cash a $1000 dollar check will incur a 3-5% fee from a check cashing center. That's an average of $40 in fees for a single check! Even if a bank charges $10 per month for a checking account, you can cash way more checks and ultimately spend much less!

Oppositions of check cashing centers assert they exploit the consumers they serve, while providing a facade of convenience. A little known fact is that even for those individuals who are unable to open a checking account; there are alternatives, such as second chance bank accounts, which provide users the convenience of a checking account without having to pass any type of credit check.

HOW DO I KNOW MY MONEY IS NOT SAFER WITH ME THAN IN A BANK?

If you have money deposited in a checking or savings account at a financial institution such as a bank or credit union, it is almost always safer than you keeping it at home in the cookie jar or under your mattress. The purpose of The Federal Deposit Insurance Corporation (FDIC) is to promote and preserve public confidence in the U.S. financial system. Both brick and mortar and virtual/online banks are protected by the FDIC which guarantees bank deposits up to $250,000 per depositor per bank through the year 2013, after which time the limit is expected to return to $100,000 per depositor per bank. It's important to note that since the start of the FDIC on January 1, 1934, no depositor has lost a single cent of insured funds as a result of a bank failure. The rare potential of a bank going out of business is no reason to not open and actively utilize a checking account. If something extreme were to take place, I'm 100 percent certain that you would be covered!

The National Credit Union Administration (NCUA) is the equivalent of the FDIC for all federal and most state-chartered credit unions.

For more information about either agency, please visit www.fdic.gov or www.ncua.gov.

I WENT AWAY TO SCHOOL AND MY BANK BACK HOME DOESN'T EXIST HERE. WHAT SHOULD I DO?

Open an account with your school's credit union. If your school doesn't have its own credit union, open one with the local community's credit union. Now that you are a resident there, you should be eligible for membership.

If you are unfamiliar with credit unions, see "*What's the Difference Between a Credit Union and a Bank?*" I believe that credit unions are a great start for college students becoming financially responsible because the learning curve will work in your favor should you make any mistakes along the way.

In addition, you shouldn't waste time being assessed fees by using a card attached to a bank with no local access. If your home bank is more convenient for your parents, either have them wire you money for your allowance or simply send you checks in the mail. At this age, you need the experience of actively using an account, as well as building relationships within your local financial institution. Local bankers and tellers may be the people who end up holding your hand through any financial blunders and whom will also have the power to reverse fees from time to time for a familiar and friendly face.

WHAT'S THE DIFFERENCE BETWEEN A CREDIT UNION AND A BANK?

There are several distinctions between a credit union and a bank. It is up to you to perform your due diligence and assess which one will work best for you.

Use a local credit union instead of a large bank if you can. Fees are generally lower and the interest you can earn will be higher.

- **Credit unions are member-owned.** Once you establish an account at a credit union, you become a part owner. That doesn't mean you can walk in a branch and do whatever you want, but it does mean that you receive higher dividends or interest rates because there are no private investors to be paid first.
- **Credit unions are not-for-profit.** This type of status is why interest rates tend to be significantly better, and fees fewer and smaller, at credit unions than at banks. Again, any profits credit unions do make are distributed as dividends to their members.
- **Credit unions are exempt from most state and federal taxes**. This allows them to avoid the need for creative fees that many banks come up with to pass on to customers. The average penalty for overdrawing an account with a credit union is between $20 and $25, whereas with a bank, fees are usually in excess of $34.
- **Credit unions have eligibility requirements.** Practically anyone off the street can walk into a local bank branch and open a checking account – assuming they haven't damaged their reputation with a financial institution. Credit unions, on the other hand,

require members to have something in common. For instance, your college may have a credit union that only allows students, alumni, faculty and staff to become a member. Virtually everyone in the United States can belong to a credit union because of where they live, where they work or any associations they may belong to.

- **Credit unions are also insured up to $250,000 per account.** Instead of being insured by the Federal Deposit Insurance Corporation (FDIC), credit unions are insured by the National Credit Unions Administration (NCUA), which is also an independent federal agency which protects the assets of its depositors.
- **Credit unions don't usually restrict you to using their ATMs.** Most CUs either offer fee-free access to a huge network of ATMs or reimburse your fees if you use other institutions' machines.

If it sounds like I'm a fan of credit unions, that's because I am. I think they are an excellent way for college students to establish a healthy banking regimen because of the flexibility they offer their members. The minimum a new customer of a credit union may deposit is about $5 where banks ordinarily require opening deposits of $50 our $100. On average, a depositor at a credit union will receive a higher rate on deposits than he might at a bank and pay more to borrow money at a bank versus a credit union. No one has money to waste, but when you're just getting started, you shouldn't be harshly penalized for your mistakes.

WHAT'S THE DIFFERENCE BETWEEN A CHECKING AND SAVINGS ACCOUNT?

In the early days of banking, a checking account was one that you wrote checks against to pay bills or purchase products. A savings account was an account that earned interest on the amount and was paid at varying times depending on the account type. Today, many of the lines are somewhat blurred at the differences between checking and savings accounts, but they do exist.

One difference between checking and savings account is that savings accounts tend to earn higher interest rates. The higher rate comes from the fact that you are agreeing to allow the bank to use your money to make money for itself. In return, the bank pays you a certain amount of interest on the amount at predetermined time intervals. Because of this, there may be more delays with taking money from savings accounts than checking accounts. There is also a limit to how many withdrawals you can make in any given month from your savings account.

Checking accounts have both checks and a debit card linked to them in order to provide you with the flexibility of being able to make your purchases or pay your bills. Savings accounts may have an ATM card attached, but you cannot generally use them to make purchases straight out or as frequently as you may desire.

WHAT SHOULD I LOOK FOR IN A CHECKING ACCOUNT?

First of all, the concept of a checking account is really quite simple. This is the account you will use most often throughout the month to manage the money you have coming in and going out. The money going out is most often accessed by writing paper checks or swiping a debit card.

Although most banks offer several types of checking accounts, Free Checking has become one of the most popular accounts with any financial institution. Free Checking usually means that there are no fees for the account – unless you overdraft. However, it's extremely important to make sure you read the fine print. Some financial institutions may require that you have direct deposit, utilize your debit card a minimum number of times per month or some other qualifying term.

Choosing the appropriate checking account truly depends on your individual spending habits and methods, so it's important to do your research. Many people choose a bank based on what's closest to their home or the number of ATMs they've noticed in the area. While this can be right for some people, if you rarely access ATMs or even write checks, then opening an online account may be a better option for you. It all depends on your personal style.

No matter which route you choose, just know that it is absolutely imperative for your financial future that you have at least a basic checking account. Being unbanked, a person with no bank account, is financial suicide in today's modern world and has even been called economic slavery. Not having a basic checking account closes you off to the fundamental necessities of wealth building.

Remember, when completing your research on bank accounts, be sure to ask about basic information, such as fees, minimum balance requirements, overdraft protection and guidelines, interest rates (although they are not much on checking accounts) and any other questions you can possibly think of. Don't be timid; your future's on the line!

Sign up for Online Banking while you're opening the account and ensure there are no additional fees to use the service.

WHAT SHOULD I LOOK FOR IN A SAVINGS ACCOUNT?

Savings accounts are meant to help you save money, hence the name. Therefore, they come with limits, balance requirements and excessive withdrawal penalties. These restrictions will vary from institution to institution, as well as, from banks to credit unions.

The most common savings account is the basic account with a $300-$500 minimum balance requirement. Anything below this balance will usually trigger a fee; however, sometimes you can find special deals with your local banks when they want to increase their deposits. One promotion you might see is a waiver of the balance requirement if you set up automatic transfers from your checking account every month.

Along with balance requirements, many banks impose a limit to the number of withdrawals you can make a month. Generally, savings accounts are limited to six withdrawals per month, with the exception of in-person withdrawals. Anything over six will incur a fee (from the financial institution) and more than likely generate a letter explaining that if you continue to go over your withdrawal limits the account will be converted into a checking account. The fee will vary – like most others – but is usually instituted by the bank or credit union as a deterrent. However, some banks may charge a higher penalty than others, so be sure to ask about this when opening the account.

At the end of the day, your goal is to make money on your money, so look for the best interest rates you can find. Generally, you will find better interest rates with online institutions, such as ING Direct. I prefer this

Never try to save money in your checking account. That's like starting your diet in the middle of the food court. It's too easy to fail.

method if you are working on your discipline because it will take more effort to get to the money and in turn blow it. It generally takes 48 hours for a transfer of funds to hit your account. That's plenty of time to make sure what your spending the money on is actually worth it!

WHY DO MERCHANTS ASK WHETHER I WANT CREDIT OR DEBIT?

This is a great question that has only become a topic of discussion in recent years. Many debit cards, which are linked directly to a checking account, have become dual-purpose, so that they can be used as a credit card and therefore be charged by merchants using the traditional credit networks. A merchant will ask for "credit or debit?" if the card is a debit card with credit card logos. If you choose "credit", the credit balance will be debited the amount of the purchase which is then withdrawn from your bank account at a later date; if you choose "debit", the bank account balance will be debited the amount of the purchase and the money will be withdrawn from the bank account immediately.

When opting for credit, you are accessing what's known as an offline debit card. This type of transaction is available with check cards that have the VISA or MasterCard logo and can be done anywhere bankcards are accepted. The money isn't deducted from your account immediately; it usually takes two to three days. No PIN is necessary, but you'll have to sign a receipt, as well as show your identification in most cases. Albeit less convenient, some banking institutions like JP Morgan Chase will reward you with incentives for choosing the credit option over debit.

Some banks provide rewards points for saying, "credit" when you swipe which can be saved up for gift cards for gas, as well as retailers like Target or Wal-Mart. If you're going to make the purchases anyway, you may as well be rewarded!

When opting for debit, you have chosen the online debit card. With this type of transaction, money is deducted from your account immediately. It works like an ATM card, so you'll need a PIN (personal identification number). Frequently, you are charged a fee by your bank for making an online debit. Although online debits are cheaper for the retailer where you make your purchases, the bank makes more money from offline transactions, and tries to encourage the consumer to choose offline debits. Your fee can range from $0.25 to as much as $3 for each online debit transaction. Before using your debit card with a PIN, make sure you know how much your bank is charging you to pay for your purchase online.

Who knew there was so much behind three little words?

WHAT'S THE DIFFERENCE BETWEEN A CREDIT CARD, CHARGE CARD AND DEBIT CARD?

There are many variations when it comes to those little plastic cards. Their most common feature is the convenience they provide, but it's important to understand how different cards work in order to help you make wiser financial decisions. Credit cards, charge cards and debit cards may look alike, but they offer different services and benefits. Learn the basics of each card and determine which is best for you.

CREDIT CARD

A credit card is a means of buying goods and services on a line of credit. Credit cards are issued to you based on your income and other information on your credit report and application. When you use a credit card, you are borrowing money against that line of credit, basically money you don't have. You pay it back each month by the due date with interest if you haven't paid the balance in full. If you do pay your balance in full before the grace period expires (usually about 25 days), you won't be charged interest. The most common example of a credit card is the VISA or MasterCard. If you carry one of these cards, you can charge goods or services anywhere their logos are displayed or accepted.

Affinity card – This type of credit card is offered by a bank and another sponsoring organization, often a charity group or other non-profit. The sponsor's name or logo is often placed on the card. The bank typically gives a portion of your annual fee and purchases to the sponsor. Ever wonder why credit card companies can freely roam your college campus despite the concern of predatory practices? Now you know why.

CHARGE CARDS

A charge card is similar to a credit card, but it is generally used for purchases during a single billing cycle. Unlike a credit card, a charge card doesn't offer you a revolving line of credit, and you must pay the balance in full each month. The most prominent example of a charge card is American Express.

DEBIT CARDS

A debit card may have a VISA or MasterCard logo, but that doesn't mean that it's a credit card. A debit card (also known as a check card) is linked directly to your checking account or in other terms accesses money that you do have. Money is withdrawn from your account when you make a purchase, so it's more like a check than a credit card. Debit cards can also allow for instant withdrawal of cash, acting as the ATM card for withdrawing cash and as a cheque guarantee card. Merchants can also offer "cash back" services to customers, which allow you to withdraw cash along with your purchase.

WHY SHOULD I STAY AWAY FROM ATM MACHINES?

The automated teller machine was introduced in the 1960s in an effort to provide bank customers with additional convenience. Unfortunately, because of the overuse and abuse of many ATM users, banks have seen them as a prime area to collect millions of dollars in fees per year. Now, there are very few places where you cannot find one.

Although ATMs are more convenient than ever now, their fees are inconveniently higher than ever as well! Here are some tips on how to keep your ATM fees down and save the $500 per year that the average frequent ATM users spends.

1. If you must use an ATM, make sure it's a local branch of your banking institution or that you have some type of free access.
2. Use your debit card as much as possible. Not only do you avoid spending more than you need, you have a second form of receipt for all of your purchases. If you lose a paper receipt, your use of cash will basically erase your personal proof of purchase.

3. Plan in advance. Figure out what activities you plan on participating in for the week, set a budget and get out enough cash at one time to cover at least five days worth of activities.
4. Limit your visits to the ATM to no more than four times a month if you actually need to go that often.
I actually don't suggest going to the ATM more times in a month than you have pay periods. If your job pays you bi-weekly, than you really shouldn't stop at an ATM more than twice a month.
5. If you need cash and you have the opportunity to get cash back at a checkout counter, get it there. That way, you can ask for a specific mix of cash which will meet your needs and possibly stop you from overspending. Most people withdraw entirely too much money when they're at the ATM. Once they use what they actually need, the rest gets squandered away on unnecessary impulse buys.

Only go to the ATM machine once a week and make all of your purchases with the cash you have on hand. Overdraft fees add up quickly. You can never overspend with cash in hand.

HOW DO I AVOID OVERDRAFT FEES?

It's important to understand that checking accounts can be overdrawn if you're not careful. The fee itself will vary; however, the average charge is about $35. In most cases, this fee is per item that overdraws your account... regardless of the amount. So, if you have four items that come through after your bank balance has gone negative, then that means that four separate fees will be assessed for a whopping $140! Does this sound like a reason to pay attention? Sure it is. Especially if all the purchases you made were for small items. Remember, small careless decisions can often amount to humongous consequences!

You have options to protect you from this. First and foremost, it is important that you keep a register or some other means of efficiently tracking your balance. I agree that charging $35 for an item that overdrew your account by $2 is ridiculous, but if you didn't spend more than you had, you wouldn't get the fee in the first place. Take some responsibility and keep track of your finances. Rest assured that U.S. Banks take in over $38 billion in overdraft fees, which equate to more than 75 percent of the fees they charge on consumer deposits per period. As I often remind my clients, banks are not charities; they will capitalize off of you as much as *you* allow them to.

HOW TO AVOID OVERDRAFT FEES

- **Keep your Register Updated**. Simply put, if you don't know how much money is in your checking account right now, then you are at risk of overdrawing your account. Many people falsely believe that keeping a check register in their head is a good idea. It's inevitable that you will forget something. Instead, make it a habit by entering each check or debit card purchase as it is made. Set aside time when you get home to check your receipts and balance your register. Do this every time you spend, and soon it will be second nature.
- **Don't Forget ATM Withdrawals**. One of the easiest ways to lose track of your money is to forget to record cash you withdraw from an ATM. It happens to people all the time – they forget to record the withdrawal and when the bank statement comes they find out they have hundreds of dollars less than they thought. Nip this potential problem in the bud by always getting an ATM receipt. Place the receipt in a safe place. When you get home refer to the receipt to enter the withdrawal into your register.
- **Remember to Record Automatic Payments**. Having your utility or insurance company automatically take payments out of your checking account can be very convenient. Overdrawing your account because you forgot to record an automatic payment is unquestionably inconvenient.
- **Review your Statement**. The best way to keep tabs on your checking account is to compare the monthly statement to your check register. Any discrepancies need to be taken care of immediately. If you have done a good job keeping track of your money there will never be a discrepancy – and that's the goal! You can give yourself a margin for error because keeping up with the cents do get tricky at times. I like to use $2. If I'm under or over $2, I don't sweat it much.
- **Cushion your Checking Account**. Having a little cushion in your account is probably the most effective way to stop overdraft fees when

all else fails. To create a cushion, record a withdrawal in your register of $50 or whatever you want the cushion amount to be but leave the money there. Try to forget about the cushion and carry on as usual. If you get into trouble and accidentally spend more than your balance that $50 will be sitting there to take up the slack, and hopefully prevent a hefty fee.

US Banks take in over $38 billion per year in overdraft fees.They'll be fine without your contribution.

- **Sign up for overdraft protection.** Usually the protection plan stipulates that money will be taken from your savings first, and then from a line of credit given at a fixed rate. However, overdraft protection generally requires an account with a minimal balance and that the accountholder passes a credit check.
- **Check your balance frequently**. This is an absolute must if you don't qualify for overdraft protection. Take advantage of account information offered over the phone and online. With the ability to check your account information even from your mobile phone, there is really no excuse to not be aware of your balance. Keep in mind, however, that there will be a distinct difference between your available balance and current balance. Pay careful attention of the difference between these two because the latter reflects the amount in your account minus any pending transactions. Always base your spending on the amount in your ledger in order to avoid confusion and potential fees.
- **Make deposits early in the day.** Be aware of the hours in which your deposit will be processed. Usually this is before 4 p.m., Monday through Friday. This guarantees that the money is credited directly into your account that day. If you are transferring online, the cut offs are usually five or 6pm depending upon your bank.
- **Choose credit.** Run your check card through the credit system and not through the debit system. Not only do vendors often attach hidden fees for using the debit system, but these charges are immediately suspended from your current balance. The credit system, by contrast, debits your account in the order in which the charges were made on the next business day. Thus, your account activity will more accurately reflect your ledger.

- **Opt out all together.** Because of the Credit Card Accountability, Responsibility and Disclosure Act, you now have the option of opting-out of overdrawing your checking account. What this means is that your bank can switch off the feature on your debit card that allows you to go over what you have in your account, and your card will be declined at the time of purchase. The one exception to this is that pending transactions will still overdraw the account. For example, if you use your debit card as credit and sign for it, the purchase clearing your account is dependent on the merchant and when they batch their credit card items. It could take several days to clear the account. If you use your card in the meantime, forgetting to subtract out the first purchase and spend more than what you have available, that pending charge will clear and overdraw you. Again, this is why tip #1 is to keep your register updated.

WHY WOULD MY BANK CLOSE MY ACCOUNT?

Banks are in the business of making as much money off of the accounts you hold with them as possible. It is not in their best interest to close your account down unless you completely become a liability to their profitability. Your financial institution may close your account down if there is a pattern of writing checks for more than you have present in your account, a practice known as bouncing checks. If your account has fallen below the minimum balance you agreed to leave in the account for an extended period of time, some banks may also see your actions as a breach of the terms set forth when you opened your account. Additionally, if your account has been negative for an extended period of time (typically 60 -90 days) and the bank's attempts to contact you have gone unanswered and the issue unresolved, they may write your account off as bad debt, close the account and place the amount owed on your credit report via a third party collection services company.

Not maintaining a good debit history may result in a number of additional unpleasant consequences. Below are just a few.

- Your financial institution may charge you fees for each overdraft item daily, making the amount you will have to pay back far greater than the original incident.
- The place you wrote the check could also charge you a fee or refuse to take any more checks from you in the future.

- You could receive a great deal of collection calls and letters asking you to repay the money.
- Your name and account information could be reported to a check verification service, which could cause your checks to be declined at point of sale purchases far into the future.
- Your bank could report your closed account to ChexSystems, leading to other institutions refusing to open a checking account for you for years to come.

KEEPING CREDIT CLEAN & DEBT DOWN

CREDIT CARDS ARE NOT bad until you get addicted to them. When they become "plastic crack" is typically when the problems begin. They are usually the number one item to consume the financial concerns college students possess besides student loans. While credit cards are an important piece of the puzzle at this point, they are not the only one. There are different types of credit, credit cards and even debt. All may serve a purpose at some stage in your financial life, but all are definitely not beneficial for you at this particular point. An unhealthy mix of too much credit and debt may create a lethal dose you are simply not ready for. The pressure you receive to sign up for credit cards as a student may seem unbearable, but it's up to you to incorporate the anti-drug slogan of the 80s and 90s and "Just Say No." Prevent your own financial suicide. If you don't take a stand now, you can join the downward spiral that many people acknowledge began during their college years. Start now. Keep your credit clean and debt down

WHAT'S A CREDIT SCORE AND HOW IS IT DETERMINED?

A credit score, often referred to as a FICO score, is a three-digit number that potential creditors use to help them decide how likely it is they will get paid back on time. They are also called risk scores because they help lenders predict the risk that you will not be able to repay the debt as agreed. Scores are

Average Credit Score Ranges

Between 700 and 850 – Very good or excellent credit score.

Between 680 and 699 – Good credit score.

Between 620 and 679 – Average or OK score.

Between 580 and 619 – Low credit score.

Between 500 and 579 – Poor credit score.

Between 300 and 499 – Bad credit score.

generated by using elements from your credit report, as well as other sources, such as your credit application. Scores are generated at the time a lender requests your credit report and then included with the report. Credit scores are fluid numbers that change as the elements in your credit report change. For example, payment updates or a new account may cause scores to fluctuate within just days.

The designers of credit scoring models review a set of consumers – often over a million. The credit profiles of the consumers are examined to identify common variables exhibited. The designers then build statistical models that assign weights to each variable, and these variables are combined to create a credit score. Model builders strive to identify the best set of variables from a consumer's past credit history that most effectively predict future credit behavior.

Your credit rating is calculated by compiling information in the following five categories:

1. Payment history constitutes 35 percent of the rating. A pattern of late payments will cause a huge drop in your credit rating, especially if you see your score within weeks of a late payment being made.
2. The duration of your credit history accounts for 15 percent of your rating. The longer you maintain positive lines of credit, the better. This is why even if I advise clients to stop accruing new credit, I never advise them to call the creditor and close the line down completely.
3. New credit counts for 10 percent, so don't make a habit of applying for credit unnecessarily. This is especially true if you already have outstanding credit accounts that are carrying significant balances. To potential creditors, it appears as if you're attempting to make a lifestyle out of living off credit.
4. The mix of credit used is 10 percent of your rating. This measures how much of your debt is installment debt versus revolving debt. (See "What is installment debt and revolving debt?")

5. The total balance of remaining debt counts for 30 percent of your overall credit rating.

HOW DO I OBTAIN A COPY OF MY CREDIT REPORT?

In order to keep your credit clean, you have to know what's reflected on it. You should check your credit report on an annual basis because your credit worthiness can have a significant impact on your financial future. With good credit, it is easier to take out low-interest loans of any scale, including mortgages. Even if you know you pay all of your bills on time, checking your credit report consistently may alert you of inaccuracies on your credit file, or of signs of potential identity theft.

Request a free copy of your credit report by visiting www.annualcreditreport.com or contacting the Annual Credit Report line at 877-322-8228. Be aware that more than likely you will be asked to pay a fee in order to view the full report with the score. The free report is okay if you believe you're credit is in good standing, but if you've had any credit challenges or are planning to make a big purchase in the near future, it's important that you choose the version with the score. This will allow you to see where you stand and develop quantified goals. You may also obtain your credit report by contacting any of the three major credit agencies directly:

Experian
PO Box 949
Allen, TX 75013
888-397-3742
www.experian.com

Equifax Credit Services
PO Box 740241
Atlanta, GA 30374
800-685-1111
www.equifax.com

TransUnion Credit Information
PO Box 1000
Chester, PA 19022
800-888-4213
www.transunion.com

After you obtain a copy of your credit report, please keep it in a safe place. Lying around your dorm room or shared apartment space is a sure fire way to set yourself back if your report makes it into the wrong hands.

Seventy percent of Americans don't know their credit scores.
– CBS News

WHAT INFORMATION SHOULD I EXPECT TO SEE ON MY CREDIT REPORT?

Credit reports are sometimes very hard for the untrained eye to review. Study it, however, until you understand the five main categories of information:

1. **Personal information:** Your name, current and previous addresses, social security number, telephone number, date of birth, and current and previous employers.
2. **Credit History:** The majority of your credit report is comprised of information on credit accounts that have been opened in your name. Details about these accounts, including the date the account was opened, the credit limit or amount of the loan, the payment terms, balance and a history of your payment records on each account is also included. Closed or inactive accounts, depending on the manner in which they were paid, stay on your report for 7-11 years from the date of their last activity.
3. **Credit Score:** A three digit number issued by each of the major credit bureaus and used to help potential creditors decide how likely it is they will be repaid in a timely manner. See *"What's a credit score and how is it determined?"*
4. **Credit Inquiries:** Each time a third party, such as a creditor, potential lender, or insurer pulls your credit report, it is recorded on your file as a credit inquiry. Inquiries may remain on your credit report for up to two years.
5. **Public Records:** Public records obtained from government sources including bankruptcies, tax liens, collections, judgments and records of overdue child support are also recorded on your credit report. Public information stays on your credit report for up to seven years.

WHAT SHOULD I DO IF THERE ARE ITEMS ON MY CREDIT REPORT I DON'T RECOGNIZE?

It is extremely important to look over your credit report with a fine tooth comb as soon as possible. If you discover any mistakes, contact all three credit bureaus by initiating a dispute online. You can do that which each individual bureau at www.annualcreditreport.com. If you have physical proof of payment or any physical documentation, I suggest disuputing by certified mail. No matter how large or small, you need to alert them of the mistake and request that they investigate this matter and subsequently change or remove the item as needed. If you don't get a reply in writing within 60 days, don't just drop it. Send another letter reminding the credit agencies that they are required by law to investigate any incorrect information or provide an updated credit report with the incorrect information corrected or removed.

A sample Dispute Letter is included in Appendix B in order to assist you in drafting your own.

WHAT SHOULD I DO IF I'M JUST TERRIFIED OF CREDIT CARDS?

Honestly, when you realize that a credit card is just a little plastic card with your name on it and an imprint of a banking institution you take away its power. Credit cards are not evil in and of themselves. They can actually be a beneficial financial tool when used properly.

Credit cards don't have any supernatural powers. The power resides in the hands of the credit card holder.

There is a balance between using credit wisely and having a reckless addiction. Credit cards are a necessary part of how our world functions today. They are great to have for emergencies, when vacationing and for several other short-term uses. Those who never use credit can be denied a loan or credit when they have a justifiable need or use for it. Using credit establishes a history of financial responsibility. Until you establish a credit history, your chances of qualifying for an important loan, such as a mortgage, are greatly reduced. They are by no means a way of life or meant to pay for things that you cannot afford to buy.

Using credit means that you have a confidence in your future ability to repay the debt. Making a commitment knowing that there is no realistic way for you to pay it back with the given terms quite frankly makes you a liar. Not only have you lied to your creditor, but you've lied to yourself, as well.

More than likely, you will NEED credit to build creditworthiness in your lifetime. The only way a potential creditor can determine your likelihood of paying them back is to assess your history with other creditors. Do your research. Visit sites like www.creditcards.com and educate yourself on how to determine the best card for your circumstances.

I will say this as well, if you don't have a job or hefty allowance guaranteed to come in, there is no need to acquire a credit card PERIOD. Borrowing money with no plan for paying it back in less than 30 days is where most people's financial problems begin.

IS THERE A WAY TO BUILD CREDIT, BUT AVOID CREDIT CARDS?

There are several ways you can build credit if you wish to stay clear of credit cards all together, but keep in mind that the best credit scores are comprised of successfully utilizing a mix of different credit types, including both revolving and installment accounts. (See *"What is Installment Debt and Revolving Debt."*) Even if you have received student loans, they cannot benefit your credit score until you enter repayment.

Below are a few tips, nevertheless, for building credit without conventional credit cards. Remember that the only way to build credit is to ensure that no matter what method you choose, the credit line is being reported to the three major credit bureaus. If not, you won't be building credit; you'll just be wasting time and possibly money.

1. **Get an installment loan.**
   Applying for a small installment loan from your local credit union or bank may be an ideal way to begin your credit profile. Keep the length of the loan short -- no more than 24 months and make sure you are using the money to purchase something worthwhile; something that will benefit your college career such as a laptop or other sincere necessity. This method should help you build credit while limiting the amount of interest you pay. It also begins you with a small monthly payment you can consistently budget for.

2. **Apply for a secured credit card.**
   Applying for a secured version of a credit card simply means you make a deposit to the issuing bank or credit union, and you get a card with a credit limit of that amount, similar to a prepaid card.

Be careful with this method, however, because there can be many outrageous application and annual fees which eat away at the money you deposit. If you bank with one, your credit union would be a good place to look for a secured card. Try to obtain a card that has no application fee and a very low annual fee. You also want one that can convert to a regular, unsecured credit card after 12 to 18 months of on-time payments.

3. **Become an authorized user.**
   If someone you trust is getting a loan, you can ask to co-sign with them so that your credit will be linked with theirs. But only do this if you're confident the person will pay the loan off diligently; any irresponsibility on their part will negatively affect your credit score for the life of the loan. (See *"How can Co-signing on a Loan for Someone Else Affect Me?"*)

4. **Build your own payment history.**
   Payment Reporting Builds Credit is an alternative credit bureau that gathers data on rent and recurring payments for cable, cell phone, insurance, utility and other bills. This may be beneficial when applying for some limited forms of credit, but it is not necessarily recognized by all lending institutions.

DO YOU EVER ADVISE PEOPLE TO USE PREPAID CARDS?

I'm all for using any method that is legal and encourages young people to create healthy financial habits. While I wouldn't necessarily suggest a 40 year old use one, I believe that prepaid credit cards are appropriate for college students for several reasons; especially at a time when you're uncovering your financial blueprint and becoming familiar with handling obligations and responsibilities. The convenience, ease of availability, guaranteed approval and other features make them ideal replacements of credit cards, but perform your own due diligence when it comes to understanding the fees that may be associated with a prepaid card. While they can cost a small, yet significant amount of money to use, there's no way to jeopardize your credit or get slapped with never ending over-limit fees, as most new credit card users may encounter.

Here is some core information to know about prepaid cards:

1. Prepaid cards are granted based upon money you deposit. So any and everyone is eligible; even those with bad credit. There are no credit checks, no employment verification and approval is guaranteed.
2. Prepaid cards can be applied for online and approved almost instantly. And if sufficient deposits are made there may be no monthly or annual fees to be concerned with. Since, prepaid cards use the deposited money, there are no repayments to be made and hence no late payment fees and other associated penalties.
3. Prepaid cards are as widely accepted as credit cards. They can be used on the internet, over the phone and via any other method credit cards are normally accepted.
4. Since you can only spend what you have deposited, the chances of overspending are null and void. This can hugely increase your financial discipline and help build healthy financial habits.
5. Adding the money to your prepaid card account is simple if you use direct deposit, but many require that you add funds in person which can be a hassle. The chance of a hassle, however, is far better than the possibility of costly overdraft fees from your bank.
6. Prepaid credit cards utilize secured PIN numbers, granting instant access to cash from most ATM machines.
7. Some prepaid cards may report to major credit bureaus. If your account is in good standing your credit history can improve.
8. The activity and usage of your prepaid card can be tracked online or by using phone. This makes it easy and convenient to control and monitor all your spending and keep records.

IS IT OKAY TO USE DEPARTMENT STORE CREDIT CARDS?

For some, department store credit cards will have to be your initial entry into building a credit profile, but for the most part I am 100 percent against them for several reasons. In addition to the astronomical fees that often come attached to department store cards, what good are they if you have an emergency like a flat tire? You cannot use your Victoria's Secret or Macy's card at Goodyear Tires. In the face of an actual emergency, it's just worthless. Having a major credit card allows you to have access to money during the times you may really need it.

Today, more and more well known department stores are offering attractive incentives and rewards in the form of cash back and savings discounts to those who regularly patronize their establishments and use their credit cards. Despite how enticing this may seem, I advise sticking to one to two major credit cards in order to establish your credit.

For those of you that will still swear by your Nordstrom's card, here are a few things to consider before your next swipe:

CONSIDER THE ANNUAL PERCENTAGE RATE (APR)

The APR is the actual yearly cost of using the credit card and includes the additional fees or costs associated with your transactions. An important point to remember with many department store credit cards is that rewards, perks, and discounts shouldn't come at a price of high interest rates or overwhelming fees. Interest rates on some department store cards may range from 16 percent to as high as 22 percent, despite the low APR pitch that you were probably given for the first three to six months. Do you really want to start your adult life off in this type of trivial debt?

READ THE FINE PRINT

Some retailers require that cardholders spend a minimum amount, sometimes as high as $1,000 annually, before you can even begin to accrue any rewards. By that time you can find yourself riddled in debt attempting to earn a $25 gift card for your birthday.

REWARDS CARD ALLOCATION

With many department store credit cards, only a percentage of your purchases go toward earning rewards rather than the total amount spent. And, some of these merchants have deals that only pertain to customers who carry a set minimum balance on their cards.

THE BIG PICTURE

To earn even a three percent reward on total purchases would require $100 spent to earn just $3. Should you carry a balance to the next month, you may owe anywhere from $16 to $22 on average just because of interest. So, really you've just "rewarded" yourself with additional debt that you could've avoided all together by saving and paying cash.

The key to managing department store credit cards is to take advantage of the savings, but without losing out over the long term by paying extra fees. Never buy something merely to earn rewards and if you already have a department store card, don't credit more than you can pay off at the end of each month.

WHAT IS INSTALLMENT DEBT AND REVOLVING DEBT?

INSTALLMENT DEBT

Installment Debt is when you pay a portion of the total amount borrowed at regular intervals over the life of the loan. The assistance of installment debt allows you to purchase items at a competitive interest rate. The loan is paid back using an amortizing schedule or even monthly payments of a fixed amount over the entire life of the loan. At first, most of the monthly payment goes toward paying your interest down. The latter installments go toward paying your principal down. At the end of the specified time period, the loan with the highest interest is paid off in full.

The great thing about installment debt is that its consistency allows you to easily budget for the monthly payment. It also allows you to have a payoff date in sight.

REVOLVING CREDIT

A revolving line of credit, also called "open-ended credit," is made available for your use at any time. Revolving credit usually comes in the form of major credit cards such as Visa or Mastercard, as well as department store cards. At the time of application, your previous payment history, as well as income, will usually determine your credit limit. Once you use the credit card, you are required to make monthly minimum payments based on the total balance outstanding that month.

Despite how easy it is to obtain the credit or even how convenient it may be, this is the easiest way to financial ruin if you do not use discretion with your credit card purchases. The average interest rate on such cards can be 18 percent or more plus annual fees. Because many fall for a false sense of convenience, impulsive buying and a failure to compare the cost of buying with cash verses using the credit card or purchasing unnecessary items that you simply cannot afford are all part of the demise brought on by "convenience."

A concern of revolving credit is that there is no way to prepare for your future monthly payment as rates and terms may fluctuate based on the very, very fine print in your agreement. It can become nearly impossible to pay off your debt, while paying the minimum payment required by creditors and they know this. Creditors are not lending you money for charity; this is a business and their sole intent is to make as much money as possible. As you pay down your debt, the minimum payment is also reduced. This does nothing but extend your payoff period and, consequently, the interest you pay.

HOW DO I BEGIN TO CLEAN UP MY CREDIT NOW?

Transfer high interest credit cards to other cards with 0% introductory offers. Just make sure to double up on payments to get the full benefit.

1. **Make Up Your Mind.** In order to clean up your credit now and avoid falling into the same trap once you're out in the real world, you'll have to make up your mind now that you want to live a different life and moreover that you deserve to live a life of abundance; not one in bondage to material possessions. Decide today that if the average American lives paycheck to paycheck, you resolve to be abnormal.

2. **Write ALL of Your Debt Out.** List each debt you possess along with its current balance owed, interest rate and minimum monthly payment.

3. **Stop Using Credit Cards!** If you continue to add to the debt, how do you expect to get out of it? When you use cash, it makes you think a lot harder about whether your purchase is really a necessity. Cut up those department store credit cards and put a major one in a safe place for an emergency or opportunity. DO NOT call the credit card company and close them or you will erase the history.

4. **Know your Due Date!** Late payment fees can cost you an average of $40 per month. This is a complete waste of money! Paying three days earlier could have freed $40 for your savings account!

5. **Negotiate Lower Interest Rates.** Call your creditors and convince them to lower the interest rate by at least 25 percent. If you've made most payments on time and don't have any negative history such as returned checks, you'd be surprised at how many credit card companies are willing to work with you. They'd rather work with you then take the chance that you default and not pay them at all!
6. **Balance Transfer When Appropriate.** Transfer high interest credit cards to other cards which may be offering 0 percent interest for a specified period of time. Record when that time is up, in case you need to shift that balance elsewhere, but be careful to not make this strategy a way of life. The point is to help you get out of debt by utilizing the least amount of money you possibly can.
7. **Pay More than the Minimum.** The minimum payment is set up for you to carry this debt for as long as possible. As I've explained before, banks are a business – not a charity. By sheer design, their goal is to make as much money off of you as possible. By paying more than the minimum, you can cut the interest and principal down much faster.

HOW DO I KEEP THE CREDIT CARDS I HAVE IN GOOD STANDING?

If you have already begun to cultivate a positive relationship with credit cards, recognizing them as a financial tool and not a crutch, then use the following tips to keep up the good work:

Set your own credit card limit by deciding to never go beyond 30% of the credit limit issued by the financial institution.

1. Don't charge more than 30 percent of the card's limit. If your credit limit is $1,000, never carry a balance of more than $300 for longer than 30 days.
2. Don't juggle more than two major credit cards at this point. The easiest way to turn this into a negative situation is overextending yourself. With many more important objectives to consider at this point, don't bother complicating things.
3. Don't charge more than you can pay off in a month. Accruing unnecessary interest is not what builds credit, but using the card responsibly does.

4. If an emergency arises, use a portion of the cash you've saved first and put the remainder on credit, if necessary. I can guarantee you that the interest you will pay on the credit card is more than what you're earning in your savings account.
5. Pay your bills on time! If you can, set your credit cards up on an automatic bill pay system on or before the due date. This way, you will avoid the worry of any additional fees accruing for missing the due date by even one day. Make sure the date you choose is one when you know the money is guaranteed to be in your account. You don't want to incur a hefty fee from your bank either.
6. Using your cards regularly should ensure that your report is updated regularly. It also will keep the lender interested in you as a customer. If you get a credit card and never use it, the issuer could cancel the account. For credit scores to be generated, you have to have had credit for at least six months, with at least one of your accounts updated (or used) in the past six months.
7. Protect yourself from credit card fraud! Don't ever give your credit card number to someone over the phone or over the Internet unless you are positive you're dealing with a reputable company or trusted site.
8. If you believe your card has been lost or stolen, report it immediately. You will not be held responsible for charges incurred if it is reported before someone else uses it.

WHAT SHOULD I DO IF I'M BEING HARASSED BY A CREDITOR?

By the mere fact that you're being harassed, I'm going to assume that you've fallen behind on your obligations. If that's the case, to get out of credit card debt, make sure you read *"How Do I Begin to Clean Up My Credit Now?"*

Now that we have that out of the way, please know first and foremost that you are not the first to have fallen behind on your credit card payments and you certainly won't be the last. The reason that credit card companies extend credit to a young adult with no credit or job history is because they bank on the fact that you probably won't be able to pay on time and they'll be able to make a fortune, as they have, on the fees associated with your negligence and naïveté. Nevertheless, you do have rights and you should not be harassed.

According to the Federal Trade Commission's published interpretation of the Fair Debt Collection Practices Act, collectors cannot continuously call you. Section 806(5) prohibits contacting the consumer by telephone "repeatedly or continuously with intent to annoy, abuse, or harass any person at the called number." "Continuously" means making a series of telephone calls, one right after the other. "Repeatedly" means calling with excessive frequency under the circumstances.

If you feel you are being harassed by the guidelines mentioned above, you should try the following:

1. **Do not ignore the creditor**, especially when you know you are in the wrong. Acknowledge the breakdown or financial hardship you are experiencing and make an attempt to resolve it. With the number of individuals defaulting on credit cards, smart collectors will be happy to help you create a repayment plan that fits within your budget.
2. **Keep a journal** of the days and times of calls, as well as the method of contact you are receiving from credit collectors. You will need this in order to establish that the creditor's efforts are indeed "continuous" and "repeated."
3. **Notify the creditor by phone** if you do find that their contact is actually abusive. Let them know that you know your rights and that you do not wish to be harassed in such a manner and that you would prefer your communication by mail. Verify your mailing address with them and make an arrangement to handle your hardship if you still have not by this point.
4. **Notify the creditor by certified mail** if the harassment continues. A sample letter is included in Appendix B – Sample Letters are at the back of this book to assist you in drafting your own.

AREN'T THERE FORMS OF GOOD DEBT?

By now, you've probably heard a bunch of bologna about student loans being "good debt." Personally, I don't believe that any debt is good. You may find yourself having to take on debt in order to progress in different instances throughout life, but that doesn't make it good; it still just makes it debt. Your objective should always be to have as little debt as possible. Falsely terming something as "good," makes people too comfortable with thinking that debt is okay somehow. In no instance is it okay. Keep debt down and always have a plan to pay it off. The best debts are the ones you don't owe anymore!

IS IT OKAY TO BUY STUFF WHILE I'M STILL IN DEBT?

Absolutely NOT! The quickest way to get out of debt is to STOP creating new debt! This is the time to sacrifice a little. Buying "stuff" is what got you into debt at this early age in the first place. You need to use every extra dime you can earn to relieve yourself of the debt you have now. I'm not saying you can't treat yourself every once in awhile, but for heaven's sake do not go around getting deeper in credit card debt or buying items that are not an investment in your future. This is the time to get mad about the predicament you've put yourself in; so mad that your will to get out of debt supersedes any desire for more stuff.

If you MUST buy something, use cash. Credit cards are simply NOT an option. Remember, you and you alone, as misguided as you may have been, got yourself into this mess. This is not the time to take the "I work hard and I deserve it" stance. That sense of entitlement will keep you enslaved in debt forever!

PAYING FOR COLLEGE: KNOW THE POSSIBILITIES

LOANS, CASH, GRANTS AND scholarships: All ways to pay for college, yet the one that should be the last resort always ends up being the first place students and their parents run to. It goes back to the moronic idea of "good debt." Loans suck. They have to be paid no matter what happens to you financially or whether or not you even finish school. Servicing companies make sure it takes forever to do this and that you pay back thousands and thousands of dollars more than you even borrowed. Good debt my butt. Don't be average. Even if you are a senior in undergrad or planning for graduate school, it's not too late. Figure out how to borrow less in loans next year and make more use of free money. Think about what it will take to make paying for college as cheap as possible and then just do that!

IS IT POSSIBLE TO AVOID STUDENT LOANS?

It's absolutely possible to avoid student loans if you plan properly; and if you have the opportunity to, then by all means please take it! You will be so grateful you did in the long run. While you actually get to graduate and enjoy the fruits of your labor, you'll hear all the tales of your friends who may be paying up to 15 percent of their net income on student loan debt alone. Trust me, college loans can become a major handicap later on in

The average graduate owes $19,000 in student loan debt with many undergraduate students owing more than $40,000 since the start of the Great Recession in 2007.
– USA Today

life. I didn't leave the University of Southern California with nearly a third of the student loan debt that most of my friends graduated with, but then again I left with five times the credit card debt, so my debt repayment plan was no walk in the park either!

Here are a few ways you can avoid student loans:

1. **Keep Your Grades Up.** The only way that you can apply for any and every grant or scholarship that comes within your radar is to have a GPA above the minimum requirement. Being awarded free money is really a numbers game. The better your grades are, the more opportunities you have to qualify and the greater your chances for earning money you will never have to repay.

   Some people are discouraged because of the smaller dollar amounts that many grants or scholarships may offer, however, as the financially-savvy student you are, it's important to realize that every dollar counts! Any amount that you don't have to borrow is an even larger amount you won't have to stress about paying back in the future. Seek out a resource at your school that will help you navigate through the numerous grants or scholarships available to you and check out sites like www.scholarships.com.

2. **Work, Work, Work!** I believe in students working for so many reasons which I discuss when answering the question, "Should I work in college?" For the purpose of decreasing student loans, however, I think working at least part time in college is important. Many students use student loan money to provide for even the barest necessities when they can very well obtain a work-study job or off-campus part-time job in the industry of their interest. If anything, let student loans cover tuition; you can handle groceries! The discipline from working will allow you to value money with a much greater respect and avoid the handicap that many of your peers will inhibit from never working for anything. And if you're really feeling frisky, I am

always an advocate of creating your own income! (Read *"How Do I Create Cash in College?"*)

If you care too much about what others think about you, you'll never be wealthy.

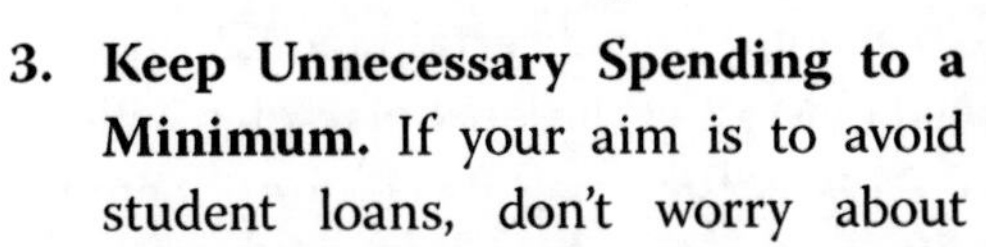

3. **Keep Unnecessary Spending to a Minimum.** If your aim is to avoid student loans, don't worry about impressing your debt-ridden friends with how much you can spend. This is not about keeping up with the Kardashians! To win in this game, remember this acronym:

WHAT'S IMPORTANT NOW!

Everything else should be secondary to the goal of getting an education without all the debt.

Implementing saving strategies now, will cut down on how much you have to repay later. Remember that for every $1 you borrow today, you will be repaying $1 plus compounded interest. And really, once you adjust for inflation and the fact that the money you earn later will be taxed, it may really cost you $3 - $4 later. Ouch!

WHAT'S THE DIFFERENCE BETWEEN GRANTS AND SCHOLARSHIPS?

Both grants and scholarships can be used to fund a college education. Unlike loans, their recipients are not required to repay the money upon graduation or at any point in the future. While both scholarships and grants allow students to pay for their tuition without having to repay, there are a number of key differences between the two.

Grants: A grant is money that is given by a non-profit organization that will generally be tax exempt. One of the best examples of this type of organization is the government; however, corporations or foundations may also provide grants to students as well. Grants will generally be given for a project, and the student will be expected to report information about the project to the donor. Grants vary widely in their requirements, amounts and expectations. They may be awarded to far more than just college students, including small businesses or entrepreneurs, as well.

Scholarships: A scholarship is a form of financial aid that is specifically geared toward students who are attending college. It is used to finance their education, and it may pay a part of their tuition, or an entire education. Scholarships will require students to meet certain requirements, both before and after they've obtained it. Most of these scholarships will require students to have a minimum GPA, and they may also require them to take a certain number of credits within the first 12 months of their schooling. Scholarships may be based on gender, major, race or any other criteria stipulated by the donor.

Despite their differences, grants and scholarships should be the primary form of payment for any college education; and loans an absolute last resort.

WHAT DO YOU THINK ABOUT GOING TO A JUNIOR COLLEGE FIRST TO AVOID HEAVY DEBT?

I honestly think that attending a junior college first is a great idea; especially for those who may have not taken the high school years as seriously as they should have and may not qualify for tons of grants and scholarships to help defray the costs. If you can attend a junior college and mitigate some of the burdensome expenses of a four-year university, as well as reinvent yourself in the grade department and really qualify for some big money, then I say go for it!

The average graduate will take a minimum of 10 years to payoff student loan debt assuming they haven't incurred any other additional large debts. - USA Today

This is not about egos. Four years will fly by. The average person takes just over ten years to pay off student loans and this only occurs once they actually start paying consistently. It doesn't include the years of applying for forbearance and deferment as most student loan holders will do at some point. Remember, your degree will look the same as the student who attended for four years, but your debt won't!

WHAT SHOULD I DO WITH A FINANCIAL AID REFUND CHECK?

Typically, if you receive a student loan for an amount more than what your school actually required in tuition, housing and other fees, you will receive some type of refund check. I have found that this is the one of the largest financial blunders college students make across the country; assuming that it makes sense to take that refund and live now on money that will cost so much more later. Please realize that this is still money you have borrowed. If money is not being gifted or granted to you, you will be responsible for paying every dime back plus interest. College loans must be paid back one way or another. You cannot include them even if you are forced to file bankruptcy one day.

If you must borrow, you should borrow the least amount of money possible. Depending on the fact that you will come out of school with a six-figure job that will erase all debt is naïve and foolish at best. If you know anyone who's graduated from college in the last 10 years, just ask them about their first salaries!

Student refund checks are issued at the beginning of every semester, so remember to evaluate this list each semester to make sure you are making wise decisions.

- **Borrow only what you need, only when you need it** - Remember that the amount you borrow is far less than what you'll have to repay. By the time you finish paying off your student loans, you'll probably end up paying around 30 percent more than the amount you borrowed (depending on how many years you take to pay the loans off and at what interest rate). Imagine borrowing $30,000, but having to repay well more than $40,000 when you only needed $20,000 to begin with. If you don't plan for this, your student loan payments may be much larger than you expected and take a bigger chunk out of your paycheck than you're prepared to pay.
- **When calculating how much student loan money you'll need, ask yourself these questions** - Can I reduce my expenses (the answer is almost always yes)? Can I work more during the school year without

Borrow only what you need and when you need it.

jeopardizing my grades? Can I work more during the summer or find a higher-paying job?

- **Use your student loan money to finance your education, not your lifestyle** - Many college students honestly believe they are managing their student loans well. They keep the money separate from their other funds and use it only for tuition, books, and fees. In reality, many students who do exactly that are actually *not* using their student loans wisely. Why? Because when you're in college, unless someone else is footing your entire bill, every dollar you spend unnecessarily will be a dollar you'll have to borrow later, which means another dollar plus interest you'll have to repay. If you can use some of your own money for tuition and books, you won't have to borrow as much.

If you MUST get a student loan refund (because yes, I realize many of you may be hard-headed), then at least budget it in a way that will set you up to win in the long term.

- **Step One:** Budget your refund. You're going to need to decide at the outset how much of your money you can allocate to expenses each month, and make sure your total expenses are less than your refund. Be realistic and write down EVERYTHING no matter how large or small you think it is.
- **Step Two:** Place the bulk of your money in a high-interest savings account. An online bank like ING Direct is great. The fact that it takes about 48 hours to transfer funds will likely be a great tool in stopping you from spending impulsively when you're out with friends or that last minute fraternity party comes up.

My ultimate advice, however, is "DON'T TAKE THE CHECK!" Allow it to be applied to the following semester or contact your student loan lending institution to find out how you can send it back. You may not get the shopping spree you want now, but think of the lifestyle you can live later while your friends are spending every penny they have on repaying student loans!

HOW DO I KNOW THE DIFFERENCE BETWEEN THE TYPES OF LOANS I BORROWED?

One surefire way to know what type of loan you have is to read all loan documents and be informed of what you and/or your parents have signed your names to. If you can't find those documents, make sure to visit the financial aid office on campus and get help immediately.
Most loans will fall into the following categories:

Stafford Loans are federal loans offered by the government and can be subsidized or unsubsidized.

- **Subsidized**: The government will pay the interest loan while you are in school and during grace and deferment periods. Students must demonstrate financial need to be eligible for a subsidized Stafford Loan.
- **Unsubsidized**: Students are responsible for all interest, although payment is deferred until after graduation. All students, regardless of need, are eligible for the unsubsidized Stafford Loan.

Private Student Loans are credit-based, non-federal student loans that can help you cover any school expenses you have remaining when scholarships, grants and federal student loans aren't enough.

Many private student loans will help you cover up to 100 percent of your school costs — not just your tuition and fees, but other acceptable college expenses like rent (or room and board), textbooks, a laptop, and trips home. Eligibility requirements for private student loans will vary by lender, but most private loan programs require you to be a U.S. citizen or permanent resident. You'll also need to be attending a lender-eligible school and be credit worthy or have a credit worthy cosigner.

PLUS Loans are parent loans for undergraduate students. They cover up to 100 percent of your college expenses with a low-interest fixed-rate. This type of loan allows parents who qualify to help their children pay not just for tuition and room and board, but for other school-related expenses, like books and fees. PLUS loans aren't based on financial need or income, so you can't be turned down for making too little or too much money.

WHEN DO I HAVE TO START PAYING OFF STUDENT LOANS?

Student loans must be paid off once you graduate, regardless of if you drop below a half-time enrollment status or leave school for any other reason. If you plan on attending graduate school on more than a half-time basis, then you may continue to defer your student loans until you complete graduate school. Most loans offer a grace period before you actually receive your first statement which requires a payment. That grace period can be six or nine months, but no one is responsible for confirming your payment start date and payment amount except for you. Take advantage of the exit counseling usually offered through the financial aid department of your college.

When you do begin to pay back your student loans, be certain that you pay in full and pay on time. Student loan activity is reflected in your credit score and is just as important as a home mortgage or car loan. The only difference is if you are truly in a position where paying back your loans becomes burdensome and almost impossible to maintain your needs, you can be proactive with student loan companies and defer your student loans for negotiated intervals until you can get back on your feet.

The grace period for student loan repayment is typically between 6 and 9 months.

WHAT OPTIONS DO I HAVE IF I AM HAVING A HARD TIME REPAYING MY STUDENT LOANS?

If you are having a difficult time making your full student loan payment on time, get help immediately! Do not wait until you get too far behind and your credit is jeopardized.

Call your student loan servicer immediately and discuss your options for delaying payments, changing your repayment plan or reducing your monthly payments. In most cases, you will be offered the following two options:

Deferment: If you meet certain requirements, a deferment allows you to temporarily stop making payments on your loan due to specific situations such as re-enrollment in school, unemployment, or economic hardship. Interest may or may not accrue during this period based upon the type of loan you are deferring.

Forbearance: If you don't meet the eligibility requirements for a deferment but are temporarily unable to make your loan payments, you may be eligible for forbearance. Forbearance allows you to temporarily stop making payments on your loan, temporarily make smaller payments, or extend the time for making payments. Interest will accrue during this period on all loans under forbearance.

Loan Consolidation: A third option often chosen by millions of graduates each year is consolidation. It allows you to take all of your small loans and bunch them into one large loan payment per month. Instead of paying three loan servicing companies $200 each, you may be able to make one payment of $300 and therefore, cut your monthly payment in half. The one catch that most don't factor in is that cutting your payment in half, will more than likely double the repayment time, as well as how much money you will end up paying back.

WHAT IS LOAN FORGIVENESS?

Loan forgiveness is one of the only ways you can pay off a student loan without using money; instead you use service. The government will take care of a portion of your debts for you if you agree to put some time into serving your country. While there are loan forgiveness opportunities for specific disciplines such as law or medical school, the most common programs revolve around volunteering.

A few examples of volunteering loan forgiveness are detailed below.

1. **AmeriCorps.** If you're willing to devote a year of your life to volunteering for AmeriCorps, an organization dedicated to addressing the most critical needs of local communities, you'll be rewarded with $5,550 to spend on your qualified college debts *and* possibly a stipend of up to $10,900. For more information, visit www.Americorps.gov or call 800-942-2677.
2. **Peace Corps.** If you want to see the world *and* pay off debt, go traveling with the Peace Corps to a foreign country and provide your volunteer service there. You'll get to defer most of your student loans until after you leave the program and additionally, you may even get some of your loans reduced by up to a staggering

70 percent. For more information, check out www.peacecorps.gov or call 800-424-8580.

3. **Military Service.** You can achieve complete loan forgiveness *and* stay in shape at the same time if you join the Army Reserve or the National Guard after graduation. You can receive up to $10,000 to pay off your loans.
4. **Teach for America.** Choosing the field of education is already a noble task in my opinion, but volunteering to be placed in the most disadvantaged schools in America is an additional challenge worthy of handsome reward. This program not only offers the option of student loan repayment, but also covers the interest on loans you have deferred during your two years in the program. Get more information at www.teachforamerica.org or call 800-832-1230.
5. **Social Services.** If you're a full-time provider of early intervention services for the disabled, employee of an agency that provides services to families of low-income communities, a full-time nurse or medical technician, or full-time law enforcement or corrections officer, your loan may be eligible for complete forgiveness. Restrictions apply, but I'd say it's worth doing your research.

WORKING IN COLLEGE: REMOVE THE OPTION

ALTHOUGH WORKING IN COLLEGE may very well be about the money for many, it can be about so much more than mere dollars and cents. Much of it is about the common sense you develop through work experience. You really don't get the value of money until you have to work for it. You really don't understand the beauty of education until you've worked a few jobs that your degree alone may grant you the opportunity to never have to do again in your life. You don't understand the importance of having a strong work ethic, discipline and good time management skills until you are forced to multi-task and hopefully master all. Don't waste the years that set the foundation for who you will become. Working in college will give you knowledge and experience that just attending college cannot possibly provide.

WHY WOULD I WORK IF I DON'T HAVE TO?

I am a huge proponent of young people working while in college, even if it has nothing to do with actually needing the money to pay for college. Ironically most students I meet don't have a problem with working, but have parents feeding them loads of crap about focusing on their studies. I think parents that deter their college students from working are hindering their child's future success because not working rarely leads to significantly

Not only are you competing with your immediate peers for job opportunities, but adults with years of work experience and international students with a global perspective. Can you really afford not to work?

better grades. At least the excuse of a job could help justify any transcript blemishes.

The bottom line is there is no experience greater than work experience. It is an important part of building a healthy work ethic, developing time management skills and understanding responsibility before you attempt to enter the workforce as an adult. Not working also ruins your chances for networking and discovering mentors, advisors and advocates who can help you further your career years down the road. Also keep in mind that many graduate schools and employers prefer a student who performed decently academically with work experience because it shows their ability to multitask. Employers will know they don't have to waste time teaching basic business protocol because you've already been trained elsewhere.

HOW CAN ANYONE POSSIBLY BALANCE WORK AND SCHOOL?

During my junior year at the University of Southern California I made the Dean's List twice. Most of my friends were baffled at how I could achieve above a 3.5 grade point average, maintain a full-time work schedule which included a start time of 5:30am, be actively involved in three organizations on campus, volunteer to read weekly to 2nd grade students, date and have a ridiculously amazing social life. It was simple; I prioritized.

The average American watches more than 4 hours of TV each day (or 28 hours/week, or 2 months of nonstop TV-watching per year). In a 65-year life, that person will have spent 9 years glued to the tube.
-The A.C. Nielsen Co.

Understanding how to truly prioritize is the key to balancing work, school and even a social life. I don't believe deprivation has to occur in any area of life as long as discipline exists. Here are a few ways you can create discipline and balance in your life:

1. **Keep a written calendar or appointment book.** As our dependency on smartphones and PDAs grows, we ignore the importance of writing activities down and being able to physically see our week

at a glance. Writing information down allows us to remember the items we've obligated ourselves to, as well as see the gaps where study time and social time can be added.

2. **Start assignments in advance.** If you always stay ahead of the game on your school work, you never have to worry about work interfering with last minute assignments. The syllabus is usually presented during the first week of school. Always stay one week ahead of it. Read when you don't have to and always start projects at least a week in advance. Even if you have to cram an assignment in, the less you have to do, the better.
3. **Choose social activities that really mean something to you.** There's no point in being minimally involved in several organizations and clubs on campus. Rather, hold an office in at least one organization and be an active supporter of another one or two. Make sure your employer knows your commitment level to and involvement in extracurricular activities upfront. Lean on the sympathy of the employer now because you won't get much post-graduation!
4. **Be okay with saying, "No."** There's so much going on in college that pressure from friends can make you feel like "you're missing out." There are so many different events on campus that missing one will not be the end of your social life. Your priority to be well rounded and accomplish more than just an "A+" in hanging out will outweigh the comments of peers who more than likely will have a difficult time to adjusting to "real life."

You can have it all: Great grades, an uber-active social life and even extra cash. It's all about believing you can, being realistic and prioritizing your schedule in a supportive way.

SO, WHAT ARE THE BEST JOBS FOR COLLEGE STUDENTS?

I believe that any job that is legal and willing to work around your class schedule has the potential to be a great job for a college student. I already worked full time as a front desk agent at a large hotel months before I began my freshman year in college. When school started, I continued to work full time and switched to a graveyard shift. I know that many of my friends thought I was crazy, but I loved my job, the interesting people I would meet and the fact that I was 18 years old and earning what the average 30 year old was earning at the time.

I know I may have been a bit extreme, but my point is you may find a job in your college town that is not specifically work study or designated for college students and make it work. What you can juggle will be totally up to you! (Read *'How can anyone possibly balance work and school?'*)

Here are some basic recommendations to get your juices flowing:

1. If your transportation is an issue, always opt for a work study or campus position first. Jobs in the bookstore or some type of administrative office will likely be the most flexible.
2. Get a job in the food service industry. Chances are high that at least you can eat for free which is always a plus in my book!
3. Baby sit. Parents always seem to think high school and college students are the best babysitters ever. If you actually are responsible, take advantage of that.
4. Apply at local attractions like amusement parks or museums. These are great places to look into when considering the need for flexible hours. More than likely, you can just work on the weekends.
5. Consider places that need graveyard positions filled like hotels. They're always open, well populated and generally very safe. Notice, however, I said "hotel" – NOT motel. The thought of a college student working in a motel gives me the creeps!

Always remember my motto: When you can't find a job, create one! Learn how to under *'How can I create cash in college?'*

HOW CAN I CREATE CASH IN COLLEGE?

My simplest answer is to use your God-given talents, gifts and abilities to create cash. There is no limit to the type of business you can create right now. From the most specialized service to the simplest task, there is someone out there that needs what you have to offer; they just have to know you are ready, willing and able to do it.

I'm providing suggestions to get you thinking outside the box, but you know yourself, your abilities and your likes better than I do. It's up to you to brainstorm and take action!

1. If you are a true subject matter expert, create a Web site or blog about your favorite topic. You can make money by offering yourself as a consultant.
2. Tutor people on campus. If there's a subject that comes to you effortlessly, be assured that there is a student on your campus who just doesn't get it. You two may be a match made in heaven.
3. Solicit graduate students for help with their dissertation research, proofreading, editing or document typing and formatting. More than likely they work full-time as well as attend school, so this could be a great help.
4. Maintain social networking sites for small businesses and entrepreneurs. What is second nature to you is a daunting task to many. You can help build their business and add valuable experience for yourself.
5. Do laundry for lazy guys and mama's boys on campus. (I haven't had anyone take me up on this yet, but I think it could be a great business! Maybe a little gross at first, but good.)
6. Get paid for your opinion. Register for focus groups, as well as online services which pay per survey or by the hour.
7. If you have a car on campus, help others run errands like going to the grocery store or even the airport. Make sure, however, that you have full coverage car insurance before allowing anyone else in your car.
8. If you love animals, pet sit or even dog walk. Do your research. You'll be surprised at the hourly rate folks pay to have someone kind and loving spend time with the furry family members.

You are blessed with a unique set of talents, gifts, skills and abilities that someone out there is dying to pay for.

No matter how small or large your business idea, write out a plan. Utilize sites like www.sba.org or www.score.org to help you determine who your target market is and how you can reach them. Create cheap ways to advertise and make it happen. In any business, if you fail to plan, you inevitably are planning to fail.

WHAT'S THE VALUE IN AN UNPAID INTERNSHIP?

As I've said, I believe wholeheartedly in working and not just because of the money. The skills you get from working, whether it is a paid position or an unpaid internship are invaluable. The great part about an internship is that it exposes you to a field and allows you to assess whether it is something you are actually interested in doing long term. The summer after my sophomore year, I did an internship in the Buying Department of a major retailer. I expected a completely different atmosphere; one filled with fashion shows and glamorous clothing. The reality was I hated it shortly after starting. Most of my time was spent analyzing spreadsheets and although I love numbers, I despised sitting in a cubicle staring at them all day. I did a great job and they wanted me to come back the next summer, but I wouldn't dare! I could've spent my entire college career chasing a job that I would've been totally depressed doing.

You can't put a price on practical experience.

Another jewel to keep in mind is that an unpaid summer internship can also turn into a paid part-time job when the fall semester rolls back around. If you were a hard worker and well received by your employer, there's no telling what the future may hold. The next internship I had after the retailer was in a radio station. It was a position I stumbled into, but I ended up staying for two and a half years until I left college and to this day, the relationships I built there continue to impact my life in a positive way.

IS IT MANDATORY THAT COLLEGE STUDENTS FILE TAXES?

You may feel like you've made too little money to file taxes, but if you've had any money withheld from your paychecks, you should have a refund coming. The rule of thumb is that if you've earned income over $900 or even received a W-2 or 1099 form you should file taxes. One of the most common errors college students make is assuming that they are exempt from filing taxes simply because they are a student. In some cases, you could be missing out on money that's actually due to you, as well as special tax considerations, such as the Hope Credit, a tax credit which helps offset the costs of higher education by directly reducing the amount of your taxable income.

Most college accounting departments have students offering free tax help so they can get some practice with real-life returns. If you haven't seen ads around campus, contact the accounting or business department and find out how you can get some advice. The Internal Revenue Service also offers in many communities Volunteer Income Tax Assistance sites where you can go to get help from IRS volunteers.

Remember to start looking into your tax situation early. If you have a lot of issues to work out, knowing in February sure beats finding out on April 14th when the deadline for returns is on April 15th. No matter what, always check with a tax professional. Unless your parents are actually CPAs, they are just adults who have paid taxes before; they are NOT professionals!

CAN I CLAIM MYSELF OR SHOULD MY PARENTS?

In many families, I realize how hard it can be to talk to mom and dad about their finances. But, to determine the answer to this question, you have to know a little about their financial picture to plan who should claim you as a dependent and possibly use your education credit or deduction.

If your parents are paying more than 50 percent of your expenses, they are entitled to list you as a dependent on their taxes. Also keep in mind that the available education tax credits will wipe out taxes that you owe, but they won't generate a refund. If you're not making a lot of money and don't owe any taxes, these credits can't help you. And the value of a deduction (for example, the higher education expenses deduction) increases with your tax load, making it much more valuable to someone in the 35 percent bracket (your folks) than someone in the 15 percent bracket (you). So unless you expect to owe a bundle, chances are your parents will get more out of a credit or deduction than you will. Don't get caught up in trying to get a $250 refund, when the education credit can save your parents thousands of dollars. Just ask them to give you what you may have gotten on your own and make everyone happy.

In all circumstances, be sure to check with a tax professional.

I'VE SEEN COMMERCIALS FOR PAYDAY LOANS. CAN I USE THEM IF I'M BEHIND ON BILLS?

The Consumer Federation of America and the Federal Trade Commission have issued warnings to consumers about the dangers of predatory lenders and the possibility of innocent Americans becoming tangled in debt through the use of payday loans. Instant payday loans are easy to obtain, but they aren't as easy to get rid of. What isn't advertised is what really happens when individuals don't repay these costly loans on time.

The average APR on pay day and title pawn loans is 250%.

The biggest problem with payday loans is when a borrower in trouble turns to the loan as a quick fix and then still has trouble repaying the loan on time. A large percentage of payday loan customers extend these instant payday loans far beyond their next pay date. How can you expect to pay the loan off in full when your monthly bills continue to accrue? If you couldn't pay your bills last month, chances are you won't be able to pay those same bills and a new debt this month. This reality usually doesn't hit people until it's too late and creates an expensive debt problem worse than what you started with.

The other reason financial experts rarely recommend a payday loan is because they are generally extremely expensive. Lenders are supposed to provide an Annual Percentage Rate (APR) for every loan, but some payday loan companies use the term "finance fee" and do not reveal the true APR. For example, a fee of $20 per $100 for a payday loan may seem as if the lender is charging 20 percent interest, similar to many credit cards. However, the $20 fee per $100 is charged every two weeks. This fee is the equivalent of 26 times that credit card interest! Payday loans can have an APR of anywhere from 250 percent to 650 percent.

Take my word for it and just stay away at all cost!

OFF-CAMPUS LIVING: MAKE IT ON YOUR OWN

IF YOU HAVEN'T ALREADY, AT some point you will get the bright idea to move off campus and do your own thing! But beware! Do your research on not only where to live, but who to live with! After my freshman year, I moved off campus and rented a two bedroom apartment that was too far away from campus with a crazed maniac who I thought was a "sweet girl." At the time, I suffered from the "grass is greener on the other side" syndrome and was too anxious to move off campus. The important topics I touch upon in this chapter were never a thought in my mind then. By junior year, I did finally master the roommate interviewing process and managed to achieve the best living experience of my college career with three people who have become lifetime friends.

Don't rush. Ask the right questions. You too may experience the shared living utopia I found. Here's to making it on your own and off-campus living!

WHAT SHOULD I CONSIDER BEFORE MOVING OFF CAMPUS?

It's important to make a budget if you are considering moving off campus. (See "*How do I make a budget?*") Working through a budget will help you identify and estimate the costs of living on your own. Once you estimate how much it will cost to live off campus, compare this to the cost of living on campus to see which option actually works out better for you. Make sure you use consistent measures; for example, to get an accurate comparison of income and expenses, you must list them all in the same terms (per month, per semester, or per year). This will require you to multiply or divide certain income or expenses in order to create that consistency.

You also want to be sure that your financial aid is not compromised by moving off campus. If you are receiving an allotment for room and board, does this allotment require that you live on campus, or is it transferable to off-campus housing? Some monies may be specifically for on-campus living expenses, so be clear about this before you make the jump. The same goes for meal plans and possibly transportation.

If the move can affect your finances negatively, perhaps you should consider holding off for another year while you prepare. Don't let your emotions affect your finances adversely.

HOW DO I CHOOSE A GOOD ROOMMATE?

Much of the success of your college career will be based on who you surround yourself with. So choosing a roommate is not a task that should be taken lightly. A good roommate will not necessarily be your sorority sister or that guy from your math class. Just because you've had an opportunity to engage with people on a surface level, you have no idea what they are really like until you have to share both a living space and financial responsibilities with them.

Remove the emotions out of choosing a roommate. This is a business decision. Treat it as such.

In order to find a good fit, you should interview potential roommates whether you know them personally or not. If you take this task seriously and sit down to interview your potential roommate, you will have a better chance of not regretting a poor decision for the entire school year. Trust me; nothing's worse than being uncomfortable in your own home or being stuck with paying someone else's bills!

Here are important questions you MUST ask a potential roommate before making your choice:

1. How do you plan on paying your share of rent and utilities?
2. Have you created a personal budget that you are comfortable with?

3. What are your hobbies or interest outside of school?
4. Are you in a relationship? How much time do you anticipate that person being in the home?
5. What chores are you comfortable with being responsible for?
6. Do you consider yourself a tidy person? On a scale of 1 to 10, with 10 being Mr. Clean, what are you?

Here are important questions you MUST ask yourself before making your final decision:

1. What do I really know about this person and their character?
2. What impression do mutual friends and acquaintances have of them?
3. If I'm uncertain about this person's ability to be responsible, am I prepared to cover their share of the bills?
4. Have I been clear about my expectations and am I willing to be, give and do what I am requesting of them?

Once all of these questions are answered, you'll be in a much better position to choose a good roommate.

WHAT ARE TIPS FOR GETTING A GOOD DEAL ON AN APARTMENT?

1. Let everyone know that you are searching for a place. A good deal can come from your friend's cousin's co-worker at the Waffle House. "Homie Hook-ups" usually work out better than any other method.
2. Be clear on what you are looking for in a place to live. How many miles away from campus are you willing to live? How many roommates are you willing to live with? Think about and write out everything you can possibly think of. Sometimes what someone else considers a good deal, may not end up being the best deal for you.
3. I ended up with a psycho roommate and an awful apartment because I waited until the last minute to decide I wasn't going back home. Start looking a few months in advance, so you have enough time to weigh all of your options.

4. Even though you have your list of must-haves, still be willing to be flexible and make sacrifices. More than likely you will only live in this place for one year. Don't act like it has to be your dream home or better yet, comparable to your parent's home.
5. Bargain with the landlord if you are dealing with a private owner and not a complex that has strict guidelines. Maybe you can agree to perform small tasks around the property for a discount in monthly rent.
6. Always attempt to find a place where utilities are included. You're already jumping into living off campus. Juggling multiple bills may be a bit much if done prematurely.
7. Make sure that when you factor in the additional transportation and parking costs, as well as having to fend for yourself with food because you no longer have a meal plan, living off campus still fits into your budget. Sometimes it can end up being much more expensive and inconvenient than you think it will be.

WHAT SHOULD I LOOK FOR BEFORE I SIGN MY FIRST LEASE?

Once you find a good roommate and adequate housing, take your time before rushing to sign a lease agreement. This is a legally binding contract and if you don't want to be sued for breaching it, be sure that you are clear about every minute detail of your living arrangements before putting pen to paper. Don't do or sign anything impulsively and be sure you check for each item below.

1. If you do not understand any part of the lease, ask for a copy of it and review it with your parents or another trustworthy adult. If your campus offers a student's attorney, make an appointment and review it with them.
2. Be prepared to have a co-signor available to sign the lease with you, as many leasing companies will not rent to a student, especially one who has not secured off-campus employment.
3. Make sure that all proposed tenants of the apartment are signing at the same time. If you sign a lease by yourself, but have roommates,

guess who's responsible for everything in the event that someone defaults?

4. If there is a possibility of having each roommate responsible ONLY for his or her portion, go that route so you are not penalized if your roommate cannot handle their share of the obligations. (Read this twice. It's important!)
5. Inspect the proposed unit before signing and if there are any items which need to be repaired, snap a picture with your camera phone and make note of it upfront. Never sign a lease without viewing the exact unit you will be renting. All model units look beautiful!
6. Once you do sign, protect your security deposit by taking tons of pictures and even a video of the unit while it's empty. This will serve as evidence of the condition of your apartment before you lived there. Do the same upon move out. College students often get a bad rap for being more destructive than a regular tenant.
7. Get EVERYTHING the landlord or leasing staff member says in writing. This includes anything pertaining to changes in the lease, deposits, repairs, etc. Everyone is friendly until a problem arises. At that point, it's just your word against theirs.

WHAT'S THE BEST WAY TO SPLIT BILLS WITH MY ROOMMATES?

Try a free site like Billster.net to help you organize shared expenses.

If this is your first time on your own, you'll finally understand some of the stresses your parents endure with paying multiple bills. Welcome to the real world! The bottom line is you must be clear with which roommate is responsible for what bill or you very well can come home from class and enjoy a night without electricity.

If utilities were not included in your rent, more than likely you'll be left to manage electricity, gas and, of course, cable television and groceries, on your own. I suggest the following:

1. No one roommate should have the responsibility of having all the utilities in their name; one person should take gas, another electricity, etc. Whoever is in charge of a particular utility is

responsible for having it turned on and off, telling each person how much they owe and sending in the payment on time.

2. Devise an agreement on how payments will be split amongst roommates. The most common way is to simply divide each bill by the number of people living in the house. If someone uses their own personal Internet card and doesn't rely on the Internet package that comes with the cable, be sure to deduct that amount from the entire bill and only split amongst those that utilize this feature.
3. Put your decisions in writing somewhere in the house where everyone can be reminded of what their responsibilities are. That way it's no secret or surprise later to those who develop selective amnesia.
4. Post how much each person owes as soon as a bill comes in. It is courteous to give your roommates as much time as possible to come up with the money. Remember, if a utility is in your name, a late payment will be your responsibility. Even if you have to wait on a roommate's share of the money, it's in your best interest to still pay it on time.
5. If you don't feel responsible enough to manage collecting money on time from everyone and making the payment in a timely manner, at least have the payments set up on automatic payment from an account you know will ALWAYS have the money.

HOW DO I DESIGN MY APARTMENT ON A DIME?

Decorating your apartment is nothing to go into debt over. Setting up your first apartment will seem expensive or overwhelming just because you need a lot more of the basic items typically supplied with on-campus housing. Keep in mind, however, that this is not your dream home. If at any time in life, this is the time to adapt a minimalist attitude and acquire just the necessities. This apartment is just some place to rest your head, shower and study. Of course, you want to be comfortable, but just know your place will become a cozy home away from home just by you adding your personal style throughout.

Don't overspend on décor and accessories. You're not furnishing your dream home!

When considering furnishings, think about how long you look at your bedroom furniture. Not long ... Your eyes are closed most of the time, and you are looking at yourself in the mirror the rest. How important is the appearance of your dining room or lounge furniture? Not very . . . You are eating food, watching television or hopefully reading a book. Are you willing to use student loans or all of your hard-earned cash on expensive furniture just to impress your college buddies? Remember, they're broke too!

The coffee table and couch I used for three out of my four years in college was from the Goodwill and cost me $75. I did no less entertaining as a classmate of mine whose parents paid thousands of dollars for her Pier 1 and Z Gallerie furniture.

1. Start by asking friends or family members for extra household items they may not be using anymore. Think outside the box. An old couch can always be covered and tables can be painted for a fresh and updated look.

2. Buy inexpensive kitchen utensils and cleaning supplies at a local dollar store.

3. Utilize Craigslist! This is my all-time favorite site to find second-hand furniture. I'm always pleasantly surprised at the awesome deals I score on name brand, quality pieces. But don't go looking at furniture at some random person's home by yourself. No deal is worth your safety.

4. Visit the clearance center at your local furniture warehouse. They often carry very gently warn floor models at 30 percent to 70 percent off. For years I was one of the people who walked right past this area on my way to the register to pay full price for items that were actually featured in that little cluttered area off to the side.

5. Remember to negotiate any and everything you possibly can. If at all possible, never go for the list price on a second-hand item. There is always a little wiggle room to work with. If you can't get money knocked off the sales price, at least negotiate for discounted delivery and/or assembly.

HOW CAN I EAT DECENTLY AND STILL SAVE MONEY?

First off, kudos for recognizing that a healthy diet is an important topic and one that many students overlook. Not only are you strapped for cash more often than not at this stage, you're also strapped for time. With papers due, campus events to plan and maybe needing a little sleep here and there, your choice in food is probably whatever's quickest and cheapest. That leaves you with any drive thru on the right-hand side of the street that happens to fall between campus and your apartment. Believe it or not, there are ways to eat well and not spend a fortune. So before you become known on a first name basis at McDonalds, try a few of the tips below.

If you pay for a meal plan on campus, use it! Most often your student loans are usually paying for this and two things are definite: You will have to eat AND you must pay those loans back!

1. Start with a realistic line item in your budget for decent food. Putting $10 under food and assuming you'll be able to make it off of Ramen noodles and tap water sets you up for a failed budget from the start.
2. Save money by buying in bulk and splitting food, obviously, with your roommates as a first choice, but also with friends who enjoy the same items.
3. Use coupons. If you're not into cutting coupons, at least check out the ones offered in the store and if an item you use frequently comes with coupons inside, save them. You're going to buy the item again anyway. You may as well save some money!
4. Try store brands. They are often a better bargain than national labels and the quality is just as good. You'll be surprised to know that several of your favorite name brands and store brands are made by the exact same manufacturer. Check the labels next time you have a chance.
5. Keep your eye on unit prices. Don't blindly assume the store wants to save you money. They set things up to appear like a good deal. It's up to you to make sure it is by comparing how much you actually get for how much you spend.

6. Get your fruits and veggies from a farmer's market. Everything will be fresh and maybe even negotiable if you make friends with the right vendors.
7. Purchase a small campus meal plan. This way you have the option of eating some meals on campus. If you go this route, make sure that the plan is flexible or is set up around your class schedule. I had a meal plan I could never use because I was always at work or in class during the designated times. What a waste!

If you must eat out, find or create a list of local places that offer discounts when you show your school ID.

The issue of eating healthy may not be very important to you when you are young, but the damage you do to your body adds up over a lifetime, so it's a good idea to eat decently and stay healthy now. Fast food may be inexpensive, but bad for your health and thus expensive in the long run. Cooking your own food means that you can control what goes into your body and save money both in the short and long term.

HOW CAN I SAVE ON TRANSPORTATION COSTS NOW THAT I LIVE OFF CAMPUS?

When I moved off campus, the worst mistake I made was not factoring in where I would park. Even once I purchased a parking pass, I opted for the cheapest parking structure and ended up having to park so far away from the campus that I would either be late to class or get a ticket for parking in a closer space.

If possible and easily accessible, utilize public transportation. It's cheap and requires much less maintenance on your part.

Consider whether you'll need to pay for parking once you move off campus. Plan in advance and purchase the parking pass that makes sense for where your classes and activities are located. Don't skimp in this area. Paying parking tickets are costly and parking illegally could get your car towed. Both options will only result in the high fees you were trying to avoid in the first place.

IF IMAGE IS EVERYTHING, HOW CAN I STILL LOOK GOOD ON A COLLEGE STUDENT'S BUDGET?

As the self-proclaimed "queen of financial fitness and everything fabulous," I totally understand the desire to look good. It's a part of building the image and brand that will take you into your life and career. Nevertheless, I am a diehard advocate of looking good on a budget; especially if you earn the average student's salary of next to nothing.

If you care too much about what others think about you, you'll never be wealthy.

Here are some tips for keeping up the image, while keeping costs down:

1. Buy second-hand. I know, I know. That's my answer from clothes to furniture, but it's so true. You can find excellent, gently-worn pieces at your local thrift shop or consignment store. The beauty of shopping in these types of environments is that you'll be able to find one-of-a-kind gems and make them your own.
2. Never spend a fortune on trendy pieces. Invest a little more in the quality of your classic pieces; those that you can use throughout your college career and beyond.
3. Learn how to sew. Okay, well even if you don't learn yourself, try having older pieces altered and recreated into head turning, one-of-a-kind works of art. It can be much more cost effective to freshen up a dress, then by a new one.
4. Take care of what you already have. Get it dry cleaned if it's dirty and darned if it's torn. And for heaven's sake don't sleep in your good clothes!
5. If anything, spend more on trendy accessories. You can make the same outfit look a dozen different ways with simply changing your jewelry, handbag and shoes.

HOW CAN I BE FRUGAL AND STILL HAVE FUN?

There are tons of ways to have a great time in college and beyond that don't have to involve spending tons of money at all. In fact, there are several on my list that don't have anything to do with money. Have you tried these?

Join a club or intramural sport. You'll be able to exercise and socialize!

1. Act like a tourist. Check out the museums and tours your town has to offer. Learn about the city you call home for right now and see it from a different perspective. You're guaranteed to meet interesting people and learn cool, random facts you can impress your friends and family with. Remember, learning doesn't only have to take place in the classroom.
2. Host a game night at your place. Invite friends over to play their favorite games. From card games to board games, if everyone brings their favorite game, you'll have a variety that everyone is sure to enjoy. In addition, get each person to chip in a few bucks for pizza and drinks. Believe it or not, these types of events will create the best memories. Hands down!
3. Try out collective coupon sites like www.Groupon.com or www.LivingSocial.com. You can find great coupons on everything from spa treatments to that cool new local restaurant you've been dying to try. Get rid of the shame of utilizing coupons. Why should you feel bad for paying less and getting the exact same experience as the guy paying full price? Will your food taste any worse because of your coupon?
4. Host a movie night. Invite friends over for a movie night. Keep it simple and don't even mention cooking. Pop all the little bags of individually wrapped popcorn in your little box, have some dollar store candy and drinks and enjoy your Netflix subscription with your friends.
5. Any major sport events coming up? When I was in college, my roommates and I were famous for our fight parties. Way before text messaging and Facebook invites, we could pack our house out with less than 10 phone calls. It never failed. We'd have tons of friends over and all we did was chip in a little extra

Pick up a local newspaper and check upcoming events for freebies: concerts, arts and crafts fairs, theater, festivals, art galleries, and museums.

on the cable bill to order the fight. Our guests knew there was no entrance without an edible contribution to the festivities.

6. Hangout during happy hours. You have to eat anyway, but if you must go out, try to time it so that you can get the same food for the least amount of money possible. The menu may be limited, but you'll always find something you like!

HOW DO I SAVE MONEY ON TEXTBOOKS?

In order to leave college with the least amount of student loan debt, you'll have to get creative when it comes to purchasing books. Here are some quick tips to save money on textbooks:

1. Don't buy books before the school year starts. I know that sounds like you'll be unprepared, but really, you may find that your professors don't even plan on using a particular book very often. Once class starts, you can ask the professor directly what the most important books for the class are and get their opinions on which books could possibly be shared with a friend.
2. If you can help it, never buy a brand new textbook. Always look for used textbooks on campus. Network with upper classmen. More than likely you can borrow a book from a friend that has it or rent it from a friend for the semester at an extremely nominal fee.
3. If you can't rent your book from the campus bookstore, try Web sites like www.Chegg.com or www.half.com. If you find that renting the book is difficult perhaps because it's a first edition, then attempt to purchase from a site like www.Amazon.com. Even with a cost for shipping, Amazon may still beat your campus' bookstore prices.
4. If possible, search for soft-cover versions of the book instead of hardcover. There are instant and significant savings between the two. Just make sure you take care of soft-cover books so that they don't look overly worn by the time you attempt to resell.
5. Download textbooks electronically. If you do most of your work on a laptop anyway and don't mind reading books in an electronic format, try purchasing them as downloads. Doing so can cut your

cost up to 50 percent and save you tons of physical space. The only drawback would be that you won't be able to resell a physical book, but let's face it; you hardly make much doing that anyway. My favorite site for electronic books is www.cengagebrain.com.

Ask an upper classmen or friend in that major if they have used the book in the past and borrow it from them or even rent it for a nominal fee.

6. Borrow a sample copy. Professors usually receive multiple textbook sample copies from publishers who want the professor to choose their book. Can you guess what usually happens to these copies? They usually are thrown away or they sit in the professor's office collecting dust. If you see a book on your required list, more than likely there's a chance your professor has one of these sample copies lying around somewhere. Don't be ashamed about asking to use it for the semester. Be bold. Chances are your professor wouldn't mind at all. Just be genuine about your financial position and promise to take great care of it.

FROM BEAMERS TO BUCKETS: ALL ABOUT YOUR FIRST CAR

NO MATTER WHAT STAGE OF life you find yourself in, the car buying process can be a tricky task. But, with the purchase of your very first car, it's even more important to take your time, plan, strategize and try to make the wisest decision you can. Even if you were fortunate enough to come to college with a car, you may be like me and a couple of my knucklehead friends; we did everything from lock our keys in the trunk at a party 30 miles from campus to hit a parked car (that was my friend, of course!)

One of my favorite sayings is "*how you are in one part of your life, is probably how you are in every part of your life.*" At this point in your life, a car is more than likely your single greatest asset. It is also likely the single biggest responsibility you have, so how you deal with automobile issues now may be a clear indicator of how you deal with large responsibilities. The decisions you make in your car buying process, car insurance, maintenance and other details may be a great example of how you will handle other serious areas of your life. So, whether you are rolling in a beamer or bucket, take your time and learn all about your first car. Remember, this may be about more than just a car; it could be about your life.

SHOULD I PURCHASE OR LEASE MY FIRST CAR?

Definitely purchase your first car. It doesn't have to be the car of your dreams. It doesn't have to be the beauty on the lot. Your first car, and any car for that matter, just needs to get you from school to home, school to work or home to work. Right now, your transportation triangle really shouldn't be concerned with going past those three critical points. However much you can save, earn and beg your parents for should be the budget you utilize to find a safe and dependable car. In no way am I a proponent of the monthly stress that comes along with a car note. More students drop out of school each year because of being burdened by financial responsibilities then by not achieving the grades they need. If you ever have a tough time with your financial obligations, please let the money be for college and not for a car note. Despite how far you can drive, you won't be getting anywhere quickly today without your education.

The value of a new car decreases by 15 – 20% as soon as it leaves the dealership.

Leasing a car in college is probably one of the worst mistakes you can make financially. Although there are several reasons I personally disagree with leasing at the top of my list is the fact that a lease gets you in the mindset that car payments are normal. Guess what? To the wealthy, they're NOT! Why start out life with having to budget in a car payment? If you never paid a car payment and the average car payment in America was $350 a month, putting that $350 a month in a mutual fund that made 10 percent would become $791,171 in 30 years. Having to not worry about potential "maintenance costs" is absolutely, positively no comparison when you think about your ability to build wealth over the long haul.

WHY WOULD I BUY A USED CAR IF I CAN AFFORD A NEW ONE?

Who told you you could afford a new car? Let's get one thing understood up front: If you have student loans then you cannot afford a new car. A dealership may qualify you for a new car, but realistically you don't have the money for a new car if you didn't have the money to invest in your own education first and foremost.

Second, new cars aren't worth much of anything once your drive them off the lot. The value of a new car diminishes 15 – 20 percent as soon as it leaves a car lot according to www.SafeCarGuide.com. It immediately loses its "new car" designation, as well as the value of all the mark-ups placed on it from the dealer. Most depreciation takes place in the first five years. On average, cars will lose 65 percent of their value within the first five years which means that if you purchase a car that is nearing five years old or older, as long as you keep it in mint condition with low mileage, you may be able to sell it for close to the same amount you purchased it for later on.

Because of the depreciation, a new car sitting in the driveway costs more than gas, maintenance, insurance and financing combined. A problem used cars won't typically present. You can get a perfectly good car that someone else has leased and taken immaculate care of for at least 25 percent less, so why pay more? Vehicles should not have a total value that exceeds half your annual income. The maintenance alone will kill you!

Remember a dealer is at the dealership to make money and earn their own living. They are banking on you being more interested in keeping up with Kardashians, than in you actually being informed and making a wise decision that will support you in the long run.

WHAT TIPS DO I NEED TO KNOW WHEN BUYING MY FIRST CAR?

There is a lot to consider when you approach the exciting task of purchasing your first car. The first tip is to be excited, but not anxious. Being too anxious will deter you from making a wise decision that will benefit you in the long run. Many people, even "seasoned" adults, confuse wanting the lowest price with obtaining the best deal. Take your time and do your homework. Being in a hurry can cost you greatly.

1. Know your requirements. Realistically sit down and get clear about your price range, monthly budget, dependability, safety, etc.
2. Use the Internet to select the brands which meet your requirements. Don't fall in love with a car first and then tweak your requirements to fit your dream car. This is the surefire way to end up overspending.
3. Use online sites to price these models and come up with an average price you can present your local dealer with later.

4. Review the trade-in value using Kelly Blue Book or www.kbb.com. If you look under "Used Cars" you'll get an idea of the current value, plus an idea of what you'll be able to sell the car for after college if you need to.
5. Assess whether you can realistically afford the car you want. Will the car fit into your budget without you having to sacrifice too much of the other expenses you already juggle? If so, you may need to find an older model OR find a car with similar features in a less expensive brand. (A rule of thumb is your payment will be about $20 per $1,000 for whatever you borrow. So, a $25,000 car can cost you about $500 per month depending on your credit rating.)
6. Call the dealerships in your local area offering the vehicle you want and see if they offer any other benefits such as free car washes or road-side assistance, you can take advantage of. Knowing these upfront can help you mitigate some costs down the road.
7. Don't fall in love with a red car if you can get the same car in black for thousands of dollars less. You need to get from point A to point B. More than likely this is not the car you will have for the rest of your life, so don't be concerned with trivial details like paint color.
8. Call local banks in your area and ask how they dispose of repossessed vehicles. They may have a repo auction in your area.
9. Look in the local paper or Craigslist for private owners selling their cars. They are usually very motivated and willing to negotiate. Also remember, people are inherently kind. They make take less from a college student if they feel like they are blessing you, but always have an adult present who can help you perform your proper due diligence.

IF I HAVE TO FINANCE MY CAR, WHAT TERMS SHOULD I BE AWARE OF?

Here is a glossary of some of the more common terms you are most likely to encounter when you finance a car through a bank, credit union or car dealership.

APR: The *Annual Percentage Rate* is related to, but slightly different than, the interest rate. This is the interest rate times the number of periods in the year. If an interest rate is four percent quarterly, the APR would be 16 percent. The APR supposedly makes it easier to compare different loans because it always translates the loan to a yearly figure. But some experts caution putting too much stock into the APR because hidden fees can raise or lower this figure.

Balance: The balance of the loan is the amount remaining to be paid. Each time you make a payment, the balance is reduced. Take note, however, that most initial payments will be paying mostly interest. The principal doesn't begin to reduce significantly until you're approximately halfway through the loan.

Credit: This word is loosely used in a number of ways. In the financial world, it means your ability to borrow money. If someone says, "She has strong credit," it means a lending institution would gladly lend you the money to purchase a vehicle.

DMV Fees: When buying a car at a dealership, you have to register it and pay for license plates before you can drive it away. These various fees are referred to as *DMV fees.* These costs might also be called *title and license fees.* These fees are a percentage of the purchase price of the car and will slowly decrease as the car ages and loses value.

Down Payment: When someone buys a car and finances it through the dealership, they are usually required to make a down payment of cash. This payment is credited against the balance of the loan. In other words, if you are buying a $20,000 car, and putting down $3,000, the loan will be for $17,000. People wishing to reduce their monthly payments can do this by increasing the down payment.

Finance and Insurance Office: When you buy a car at a dealership, you negotiate with the salesperson. Once a deal is reached, you are escorted into the Finance and Insurance Office where the contracts are drawn up and signed. This is sometimes called *F&I.*

Finance: If a car is "financed", it means you are borrowing money -- either as a loan or a lease -- to pay for it as you drive it. Instead of financing a car, you could buy it outright with cash. When you buy a car with cash, it immediately becomes yours. When you finance the car, the bank owns it, and holds the title, until you've made the last payment.

Four-Square Worksheet: A standard form, used at many dealerships, to help the salesperson keep track of the four elements of a deal as he negotiates with the customer. The squares allow him to jot down offers and counter offers for the trade-in, the price of the car, the down payment and monthly payments.

Interest Rate: When money is borrowed, the lending institution, often a bank, charges a fee for this service. Interest rates are charged as a percent of the amount loaned and will vary based on your individual credit rating.

Lease: If you lease something, such as a car, you don't actually own it. You pay a monthly fee to *use* the car. At the end of the lease, you return the car and owe nothing more (assuming it is returned in good condition and with the agreed-upon mileage).

Lending Institution: Any company that loans money is a lending institution. It's sometimes thought that only banks loan money, but this isn't true. Auto loans can be arranged by credit unions, banks or the auto manufacturer itself.

Sales Tax: When someone buys an item, they are charged a percentage of the purchase as state sales tax. The actual percentage varies widely from one state to the next and, often, within the state. The sales tax is often made up of a state tax and a local tax. These two are combined for one grand total. On small items, the sales tax doesn't seem significant. But when purchasing a car, it can be a large factor that effects the total cost of ownership.

Term: This is the length of the loan, usually stated in months. Common terms for car loans and leases are 36, 48 or 60 months.

Title: A title is a legal document providing specific information about the vehicle and stating who owns it. If you borrow money from a bank to get a car, the title will be held by the bank until you make all the agreed-upon payments. Once you have paid the car off, the bank will transfer the title to you.

For the complete list of car buying terms, visit:

http://www.edmunds.com/advice/finance/articles/47361/article.html

WHY IS ROADSIDE ASSISTANCE SO IMPORTANT?

Personally, I don't believe anyone should be driving without the peace of mind that roadside assistance provides, but I believe in it so much more for college students.

Real TALK

It's better to have roadside assistance and not need it, then need it and not have it!

My mom has been a member of the American Automobile Association, more commonly known as "Triple AAA" for at least 25 years and I think between my freshman and junior years in college, I used all of both our annual allowances for calling on them. She had never, ever done that before adding me to her policy when I went to college. I'm not sure what happens to us in college. We go to college to learn and become more intelligent, but somehow along the way, we get a little stupid and lose our minds. I locked my keys inside my car once. I just plain left them in the ignition. The next time, I locked them in a trunk at a party on campus about 30 miles away. I had at least three flat tires which were probably my own fault; and then I don't know how many friends had to use it because their parents hadn't bothered to guarantee them "peace of mind."

For an annual fee of less than $100, you can take advantage of otherwise costly towing services, battery and flat tire service, as well as locksmith expenses. A traditional auto locksmith can cost you an average of $150 per lockout. An annual membership for road-side assistance will more than pay for itself with one incident and trust me you *will* have an incident with your vehicle sometime during your college career!

WHAT IF I CAN'T AFFORD CAR INSURANCE?

What a great simple question with a great simple answer: If you can't afford car insurance, you can't afford to be on the road! Car insurance is not optional. It is the price you pay for the convenience of private transportation. If you can't afford car insurance and your parent's won't pay it for you, you should either not have a car in the first place OR resolve not to drive the car and rely on public transportation until you can get it.

Car insurance means having to pay a deductible if you're in an accident. Not having car insurance means easily facing court dates, fines, license suspension and lawsuits.

I understand that you may have obligations and legitimately feel like it is okay to drive since you're going to school or work, but it's really not! It's a dangerous practice and should an accident occur not only could you ruin your own life, but you can make someone else's a living hell.

The National Highway Traffic Safety Administration estimated that the cost of teenager car accidents is more than $40 billion a year. During the first 500 miles a teenager drives, crashes are 10 times more likely than for an adult driver and with the increase of text messaging and constant updating of social networking sites like Facebook and Twitter, the numbers only continues to climb. Currently, your demographic makes up about seven percent of licensed drivers, but it accounts for upwards of 14 percent of fatalities in accidents. Even without factoring in fatalities, the mere collateral damage of "fender benders" caused by young people under the age of 21 is staggering. Driving without insurance can cost you and/or your parents everything. If you can't afford insurance, yet, please do yourself and everyone else a favor and do not drive.

SHOULD I TAKE OUT A CAR TITLE LOAN TO PAY FOR COLLEGE EXPENSES?

There is nothing wise about taking out a car title loan! I know you've seen the commercials, but understand that ALL advertisements are designed to "look" good and sell a service or product. Do your research. Read the fine print. The interest rates and terms on these type of loans sound great when you're desperate, but what happens when you begin to realize that you're paying back way more than you borrowed? By that time, they own the car that you, or more than likely your parents, worked so hard to provide for you. Don't do it. Big mistake!

A title loan offers you cash from the lender and in return you sign over the title of your paid-for car to secure the loan. Typically, these loans are due back in full 30 days later. There's no credit check and only minimal income verification.

It sounds pretty straightforward, but borrowing from these places can lead to a repossession of your car and a whole lot of financial trouble. Car title loan companies are known for having interest rates that would make a credit card company blush! While the average interest rate on a credit card may be in the mid to high teens, the APR on title loans can reach triple digits. A past client of mine had an agreement which showed a 250 percent APR (Don't see the monthly APR of 20 percent and think you're ahead of the game. Look at the total life of the loan to get realistic numbers.)

In addition to high interest, these car title loans usually include a number of fees that add up quickly. They have been lumped into the "predatory lending" category by many consumer protection organizations across the country. The fees include processing fees, document fees, late fees, origination fees and lien fees. The cost of all these fees can be anywhere from $80 to $115, even for just a $500 loan.

I gave you all this background for your reference, but the basic answer is simply, "NO!" I once read a report that shared one woman's horror story. She paid $400 a month for seven months on an interest-only payment term for a $3,000 loan. After paying $2,800 in interest, she still owed the original $3,000 in the eighth month.

If you find yourself contemplating a car title loan, check out these alternative options and read the information for yourself at www.responsiblelending.org or www.consumerfed.org.

The average APR on pay day and title pawn loans is 250%.

RELATIONSHIPS & MONEY:
MANAGE YOUR MONEY LANGUAGE

MONEY HAS ALWAYS HAD a way of coming in between some of the tightest bonds and relationships in nature. If you've ever sat through one daytime court TV show, you've seen children suing their parents, brothers suing sisters or neighbors and best friends engaging in heated and hurtful debates over money. A money-etiquette survey in 2007 states that "57 percent of people said they have seen a friendship or relationship ruined because one person didn't pay back the other."

If you haven't experienced any such drama in your life, the following pages will offer tips on how to avoid it as much as possible. However, the reality is that at some point you may face one of these awkward and potentially hurtful scenarios. Does that you mean you avoid it like the plague? Does that mean you don't discuss differences in order to avoid fighting? No and no! It means that you learn how to communicate about money effectively. You can't have a great relationship with anyone on any level until you learn how to effectively talk about money. Is it always an easy task? Not at all! But, not learning how to manage conflicts and conversations around money and potentially losing family members and good friends won't be easy to handle either. The choice is yours.

SHOULD I LEND MONEY TO FRIENDS?

Never lend money that you can't afford to give. Loaning money to your friends, or even family, is a really bad decision when you are not truly in a position to do so. If you want to lend money to someone in need, you may as well as consider it a gift and let go of any thoughts that you may get the money back. If they repay you, great! If they don't, then there should be no love lost because your primary concern was helping them out and you did that.

Never lend money you can't afford to give.

The problem with some folks is that they will keep coming back once they realize how "generous" you are. My mentor in college, author & comedian Steve Harvey, always says, "The best thing you can do for a poor person is *not* become one of them." I wholeheartedly agree. Learn now to say "NO" and teach your friends and/or family members how to do just what you are learning how to do; take *personal* responsibility for their *personal* finances.

If you still decide to lend money to someone, at least take a few precautionary steps to help protect your interests:

1. Be clear about what the money is for and be sure there are no other alternatives you can help the borrower come up with.
2. Put the terms in writing so that all parties involved understand that this is a loan and not a gift. Include a repayment plan, repayment date and outline consequences for nonpayment.
3. Set up a system and date for repayment. Either agree to accept a realistic number of equal installments or determine a date when all funds should be made payable.
4. If possible, make sure the agreement is made with someone else present as a witness.
5. Always leave a paper trail. Give funds via money order, cashier's check or personal check. Never give cash.
6. Please reconsider and just don't lend money!

SHOULD I BORROW MONEY FROM FRIENDS?

Unless we're talking about $5 until you get back to your dorm room, then you absolutely should not be borrowing money from your friends. I'm not really a fan of lending money at all, but I'm less of a fan of borrowing money especially at this age. If you start borrowing money now, it becomes a way of life for you and eventually you become that person that everyone dodges.

You especially shouldn't begin the habit of borrowing if you don't possess a consistent income and have a solid plan for repayment. Think about why you would ever borrow money from a friend; another struggling college student. Do you think your friends can honestly afford to just give you money? I know you said "borrow", but if they lend to you, more than likely they will probably end up having to accept that they just gave you the money or you'll lose a friend all together.

Never borrow money you can't afford to give back.

Don't put your friends in an awkward position. Borrowing money makes relationships awkward. Even if you are truly in a bind and your friend loans you money, the first time they see you with something that even remotely looks new, they'll think to themselves, "He owes me money, but he has new shoes on?" I say just avoid this all together. Don't borrow from people who genuinely mean something to you. More than likely, if you mean the same to them and they are actually in a position to help, they'll just do it. If they're not, they won't, but you shouldn't make them feel bad about it.

WHAT SHOULD I DO IF THE PERSON I'M DATING IS BLATANTLY IRRESPONSIBLE WITH MONEY?

Well, first of all I applaud you for recognizing the differences in the financial blueprints both you and your partner possess. Nothing is worse than becoming far too invested into a person or relationship and then realizing that there is just no changing them.

First, I'd say to make the conversation about money comfortable for your honey. You don't want to be a nag or become overbearing, but you do want to gently show them a better way of managing their money if you're convinced that they're totally confused about the topic. Discuss their money blueprint with them. Try to gain insight into why they may appear so irresponsible with money and help they recognize what's at the root of the problem. Remember, a lot of people will *do* better when they *know* better!

Money problems and the fights they typically raise have been the leading cause of divorce for decades. Don't be fooled! However, they are by no means new. But, the good news is that money issues and all the drama they bring are 100 percent preventable. You just have to get on the same page; especially if you think this person could be "the one."

In the meantime, whatever you do, do not co-sign nor loan money to them no matter how much you love them. Almost everyone who gets into a serious relationship in college imagines that person being "the one." But, nine times out of 10, they won't be. Don't bind yourself financially to them nor make yourself responsible for their money habits, good or bad.

Remember, if you can talk about money with your honey, you'll be able to talk about anything.

HOW CAN CO-SIGNING ON A LOAN FOR SOMEONE ELSE AFFECT ME?

When you co-sign for a loan, you basically tell the lender that you accept equal responsibility for the loan. If the actual borrower fails to pay, YOU are guaranteeing that the payment will still be made, even if YOU have to make it! You're not just helping your friend or family member get a loan; you are literally promising that you will pay the debt yourself if the borrower doesn't. Studies have shown that as many as three out of four co-signers (75 percent ultimately end up making payments on the loan.

So what happens if you co-sign on a loan and the borrower defaults?

1. If the lender decided to sue and actually won, your wages could be garnished or liens and judgments could be placed against your personal property until the debt was satisfied.
2. Your credit report could be severely tarnished from several months of late payments, as well as a judgment being attached to it.
3. You may eventually have to pay up to the full amount of the debt in addition to late fees or collection costs, which will increase the amount.

If for some reason, none of the above scares you and you still are considering co-signing for a friend or relative, please ALWAYS remember the following:

1. Know the person you are attempting to help. Before agreeing to sign on the dotted line, study their financial habits and make sure you are comfortable with how they manage their own money.
2. Verify that the person is employed and what their take home pay is by reviewing their paycheck stubs and bank statements. If they don't want to offer that type of personal information, they shouldn't be asking to put your creditworthiness in jeopardy.
3. Understand your own capability. Make sure that you have enough income left over each month to pay the minimum payment on this account should something occur unexpectedly.
4. Be sure you have an opportunity to discuss all of the terms of the agreement with the actual lender.

Don't co-sign on anything you can't afford to pay by yourself.

If you feel uncertain about one or more points above, seriously reconsider co-signing. Think about the reason this person cannot qualify for a loan on their own. There is good cause for why the bank is not willing to take on that risk. If they damaged up their own credit, don't be fooled into thinking they will take better precautions to protect yours. Protecting your credit is up to you!

HOW SHOULD I HANDLE FRIENDS THAT SEEM TO HAVE IT ALL?

If you are a struggling college student, it goes without saying that you are not alone! However, it never fails that you will end up meeting friends along the way who don't share in your "broke college student" struggle. This doesn't mean that you can't maintain a wonderful friendship, understanding and respectful of each other's circumstances.

Here are helpful tips on how to deal with friends that may not completely identify with your financial struggles.

1. **Don't try to keep up!** Just because your friends can shop every weekend, doesn't mean that you should attempt to do the same. Be realistic about what you can spend, otherwise you'll run yourself into debt trying to figure out how to keep up with someone who may be doing this effortlessly.
2. **Don't make them feel guilty.** If you see your friends spending what you believe is "too much money," don't chastise them or attempt to make them feel guilty. It will make you appear bitter about your own circumstances. If you genuinely want to share personal finance tips and advice with them, then do it in a helpful and supportive way.
3. **Don't be afraid to communicate.** If your friends are not bound by the same budget you are, they may constantly suggest that your quality time is done shopping at the mall or in some pricey café. Even if you don't want to go into tons of details about your own situation, don't be afraid to suggest alternative hang-out options. Maybe you can suggest cheaper places to eat that you've heard are fantastic or get them to check out the cool new consignment shop in town.
4. **Return the favor.** If your wealthier friends start to pick up on the fact that your wallet is a little tighter than theirs, they may want to treat you more when you go out. It will be normal to want to reciprocate, but you will obviously have to figure out ways to return the favour within your means. Offer to have movie or game night at your place. You can grab pizza and soda and have a fantastic Friday night on you!
5. **Use any envy for good.** Understand that any feeling of envy you may be feeling is completely normal. You just have to find a way to make the envy eventually beneficial to you. Use those feelings to motivate you to accomplish goals that will not only allow you to live a little better off after graduation, but even to make sure your own children have more taken care of for their college experience than you may have had.

Nevertheless, never forget to keep things in perspective. You never know what financial situation a person may truly be in. I knew people who appeared to have it all, but by senior year their parents were drowning it debt and facing both foreclosure and bankruptcy.

I THINK MY FRIENDS ARE TAKING ADVANTAGE OF ME FINANCIALLY. HOW DO I PROTECT MYSELF, BUT KEEP THE FRIENDSHIPS?

I'd really hate to be the one to break this to you, but if there are people who are taking advantage of you financially or in any other manner, they're really not your friends.

If you feel like you do have a friend that genuinely cares about you, but stills expects you to help them out financially because they believe you can, try making them aware of the problem. Tell your friend that you are feeling used. Ask them plainly if they are only hanging around you because of your ability to pay for things OR is it because they truly enjoy your company.

A true friend never gets in your way unless you happen to be going down.
– Arnold Glasow

Understand there are two parties to this type of co-dependent relationship: The used and the user. You are allowing yourself to be used. Think about why you would continue to befriend a person who only wants to take advantage of you. Are you otherwise lonely? Is it hard for you to make friends for some reason? A few years ago I coached a client named Erin. She made good money as an in-home care provider, but never could meet her monthly obligations smoothly. After just three sessions, we realized that all of Erin's money was being "lent" out to friends who never paid her back; many of them repeat offenders. So, why would she keep letting them take advantage of her? She was "buying" their friendships. Erin didn't have many friends growing up because she was known as the class nerd. The only reason she made a few friends even back then was by buying people lunch. She was 32 and doing the exact same thing with much bigger numbers and, unfortunately, to her own financial detriment.

You have to discover and acknowledge the root of this problem and it honestly doesn't begin with the friend; it begins with you understanding your own value as an individual. Erin didn't need to buy her friendships and neither do you.

To find out whether or not someone is genuinely interested in a friendship with you, completely take money out of the equation. Do not lend anyone money or offer to purchase anything for them. Keep conversations pertaining to money to a complete minimum or eliminate them all together. Take note of your "friends" reactions when you have no money to offer and see how long they stick around. Those that do hang around and continue to invest in your friendship are actual friends. The others don't deserve your friendship and you should reconsider who you allow to have that title in the future.

A BRIEF WORD ON INVESTING

THE BEST THING ABOUT investing at such an early age is that time is on your side. The earlier you begin the journey, the more likely success on your journey will be attainable. Understand that the money you use to invest is NOT the money you plan on buying books with next semester. Money needed in the short term – let's say at this age, two years or less, needs to be kept in a savings account. Any money above that can be invested.

If you don't have the basics of your financial life down at this point, then investing should not be a primary concern for you. Definitely begin to think about the topic, research different vehicles and understand terminology, but don't put your book money in the stock market – just yet! In future books, I will definitely expand more, but for now here is a brief word on investing.

AREN'T I TOO YOUNG TO INVEST?

I don't think you can ever be too young to invest. Your age doesn't matter as much as how mentally and financially prepared you are to actually make long-term decisions. If you are in debt and don't have adequate savings in place, at any age, you may still be unable to invest.

Never invest in anything that you don't understand and cannot explain in your own words.

If you do have your debt and credit in order, as well as a savings account in place with at least three months of living expenses stashed away then you can absolutely try your hand at investing. Just make sure that whatever you decide to put your money in, you understand 100 percent. Never invest in anything that you don't understand and cannot explain in your own words. Don't invest in something because someone else says you should. Everyone's tolerance is completely different. While some people get a rush of excitement at the thought of investing, others may break out in a cold sweat due to nervousness.

You have to do independent research and then make an independent decision on what will work for you.

WHAT ARE THE BASICS OF INVESTING?

When most people think about investing they automatically think about purchasing stock. Stocks are not bad, but they are not the only investment vehicle you have at your disposal and they can be extremely dangerous if you invest everything in a single stock. Below is a quick breakdown of a few practical vehicles that are available to you.

Stocks – Buying single stocks is extremely risky. When you put all of your money in one company, you are risking everything and at this age, that can be extremely detrimental. Heck, it can be disastrous at any age!

Bonds – The next most commonly known investment vehicle are bonds. Bonds are basically a debt that a company has and you are the one loaning the company money. It's just as risky as stocks because if the company goes belly up, so does your entire investment.

Annuities – An annuity is a savings account with an insurance company. Annuities come in two forms: Fixed and variable.

Mutual Funds – A mutual fund is where tons of people will mutually invest in a fund, which represents multiple companies. Your risk is lower because unlike single stocks or bonds in one company, if one company goes down, but several others stay afloat, you won't go flat broke overnight.

Real Estate – As a real estate broker, you're probably thinking that I will say real estate is a great investment vehicle. . . . Well, you're right! It is, if you can invest for the long term and do it without accruing ridiculous amounts of debt. I can tell you from experience, I've been fortunate enough to make some awesome investment decisions. After college, I purchased a condo in Los Angeles from a probate estate for $160k. Four years later I sold it for nearly $300k. Not bad, right? Well, in the meantime, I also bought a few rental properties in Charlotte and Dallas. For every dollar I made on the condo I lived in, I lost about $3 to $5 dollars on the other three!

WHAT TYPE OF INVESTMENT PLANS MIGHT I BE OFFERED AFTER GRADUATION?

First of all, if your first job after graduation offers you an investment plan, CONGRATULATIONS! You better jump at the chance to take it! And don't take it and do the minimum. Do the maximum, especially if your employer is willing to match your efforts and take full advantage of the opportunity. Your second employer may not be able to provide you with this luxury!

Here's what you might see:

401(k) Plan – This is the plan you here of most often. It's a corporate pre-tax contributory plan, payroll deducted, tax-deferred, with a selection of investment options to invest in. Most plans also include company matching with a vesting schedule based on years of employment.

403(b) Plan – Very similar to the 401(k), this plan is a non-profit, pre-tax contributory plan. It's usually extended to school teachers, church staff, etc. and may be payroll deducted and grows tax-deferred. It too has a selection of investment options to invest in. Some plans may provide company matching.

457 Plan – A deferred compensation pre-tax contributory plan, payroll deducted, growing tax-deferred, with a selection of options to invest in. Most plans will provide minimal matching.

Thrift Savings Plan – A government agency, pre-tax contributory plan which may be payroll deducted and also grows tax-deferred with a selection of five managed investment options to invest in. This plan offers minimal agency matching.

Simple IRA/401(k) – A smaller company pre-tax contributory plan, payroll deducted, growing tax-deferred, with a selection of investment options to invest in. Normally there is a mandatory match which boasts considerably lower administrative costs.

Should you decide to take the non-traditional route and begin your own business, there are still investment retirement plans available to you, as well.

Simplified Employee Pension Plan (SEPP) – A plan which allows a self-employed person to contribute pre-tax up to 15 percent of their net business profit, growing tax-deferred, with a self-directed selection of investment options to invest in.

WHAT IS THE RULE OF 72?

The Rule of 72 is one of the most common equations used to help investors figure out how long it would take to double their investment assuming they already know either their rate of return or the timeframe in which they would like to reach a certain dollar amount. While there are other rules such as the Rule of 70 or Rule of 69, neither is as popular because of the amount of numbers that can be easily divided mentally into 72 (1, 2, 3, 4, 6, 8, 9, 12).

To utilize the Rule of 72, you must begin by asking yourself either of the following questions:

A. How long will it take me to double my money if I earn X percent?

OR

B. What return must I earn if I wish to double my money in X years?

USING THE RULE OF 72 WHEN THE RATE OF RETURN IS KNOWN

An investor that knows he can earn 8 percent on his money may ask question A, "how long will it take to double my money at this rate of return?"

Using the Rule of 72, you simply divide the magic number (72) by the investor's rate of return (8). The answer (9) is the number of years it would take to double the investment.

USING THE RULE OF 72 WHEN THE NUMBER OF YEARS IS KNOWN

The Rule of 72 can also be used in the reverse. An investor that wanted to double his money in a certain number of years could use the rule to discover the rate of return he would have to earn to achieve his goal. A businessman that wanted to double his money in four years, for example, would divide 72 by (4). The result (18 percent) is the after-tax compound annual rate of return he would have to earn to meet his goal on time.

CAN'T I JUST HIRE SOMEONE TO DO ALL THIS?

When you combine ignorance and borrowed money, the consequences can be disastrous.
–Motilal Oswal

Have you heard of how many entertainers and athletes have found themselves in serious financial trouble after earning millions of dollars? From tax delinquencies to facing foreclosure, many people have attempted to put all of their money matters in the hands of others and found that it usually works to their detriment. Often times, you will find people, celebrities or otherwise, who have basically paid people large sums of cash only to mismanage their own money. One reason many people are broke is because they trust other people with their money instead of being actively involved in the process.

If you're not a tax specialist or financial advisor then you'll definitely need assistance, but a hands-off approach is never the way to go. And, at this stage, you may not have enough cash and assets to warrant the fees associated with hiring someone else.

Remember, you have a tool that many who have come before you did not: the Internet! You can examine more information online in minutes, than those who came before you could find after a week's worth of research. Use it! If you need guidance, seek wisdom, but don't passively put all of your eggs in someone else's basket and expect to reap great rewards.

APPENDIX A
PRINT RESOURCES

The following books may prove to be excellent resources for developing further knowledge around what you have learned here. My hope is that by browsing through the resources below you will ultimately find the style that works best for you. Your journey cannot stop with Real Money Answers. This book is a tool to assist you with becoming aware about how to make healthy financial decisions. Additional resources will ensure that you maintain them as you move through college life and beyond.

"A unique voice on money,
I WILL TEACH YOU TO BE RICH
by
RAMIT SETHI
No Guilt.
No Excuses.
No B.S.
Just a
6-Week
Program
That Works

MORE THAN ONE MILLION COPIES SOLD!
THE
MILLIONAIRE
THE SURPRISING
SECRETS OF
NEXT
AMERICA'S WEALTHY
DOOR
Thomas J. Stanley, Ph.D.
William D. Danko, Ph.D.

RICH
DAD
POOR DAD
WHAT THE RICH TEACH THEIR KIDS ABOUT MONEY –
THAT THE POOR AND MIDDLE CLASS DO NOT!
ROBERT T. KIYOSAKI

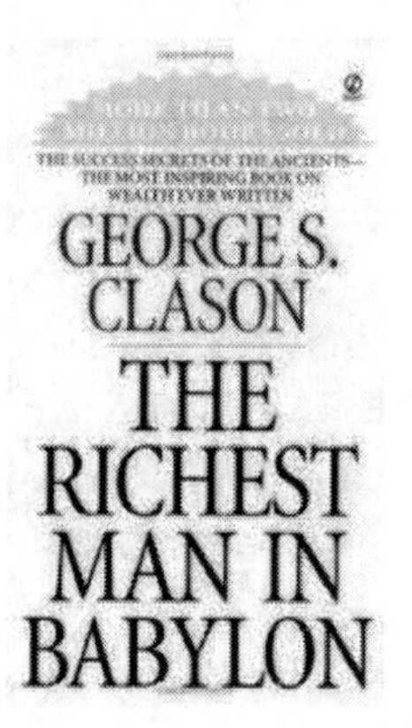
THE SUCCESS SECRETS OF THE ANCIENTS—
THE MOST INSPIRING BOOK ON
WEALTH EVER WRITTEN
GEORGE S.
CLASON
THE
RICHEST
MAN IN
BABYLON

THINK RICH TO GET RICH!
Secrets
of the
Millionaire
Mind
Mastering
the Inner Game
of Wealth
T. Harv Eker

SUZE
ORMAN
THE MONEY BOOK
for the YOUNG
FABULOUS
& BROKE

FARRAH GRAY
THE TRUTH SHALL
MAKE
YOU
RICH
THE NEW ROAD MAP TO
RADICAL PROSPERITY

YOU'RE
SO
MONEY
LIVE RICH
FARNOOSH TORABI

LYNNETTE KHALFANI
Author of the New York Times Bestseller Zero Debt
ZERO
DEBT
for
COLLEGE
GRADS
From Student Loans
to Financial Freedom
You've got your degree. You don't have to go broke.

APPENDIX B
SAMPLE LETTERS

CREDIT REPORT DISPUTE LETTER

Debt B. Gone
123 Your College Address
Your College Town, ST 01234

The Credit Bureau
Bureau Address
Anytown, ST 56789

Date

Dear Credit Bureau,

This letter is a formal complaint that you are reporting inaccurate credit information. I am very distressed that you have included the below information in my credit profile due to its damaging effects on my good credit standing. As you are aware, credit reporting laws ensure that bureaus report only accurate credit information. No doubt the inclusion of this inaccurate information is a mistake on either your or the reporting creditor's part. Because of the mistakes on my credit report, I have been wrongfully denied credit recently for a <insert credit type for which you were denied here>, which was highly embarrassing and has negatively impacted my lifestyle. The following information therefore needs to be verified and deleted from the report as soon as possible: CREDITOR AGENCY, acct. 123-34567-ABC Please delete the above information as quickly as possible.

Sincerely,
Signature
Printed Name
SSN# 123-45-6789

Attachment included. (Don't forget to provide proof if you have it! Keep a copy for your files and send the letter registered mail.)

DISPUTE LETTER TO INDIVIDUAL CREDITOR

Date

Company name
Address

Re: Acct # XXXX-XXXX-XXXX-XXXX

Dear CEO name,

I am writing to you today regarding my credit card account #4236-XXXX-XXXX-XXXX which I had while I was a student at -------------------------. The purpose of my correspondence is to see if you would be willing to make a "goodwill" adjustment on the reporting of this account to the three credit agencies.

During the time period this account was established I had was very happy with the service, I was however not the ideal customer and made mistakes with my handling of the account. I should have kept better records regarding the account and I take full responsibility. I became aware of the unpaid balance when I got a copy of my credit report in June of 2011.

I know that payment was my responsibility. I am not attempting to justify this breach of my user agreement. I was, however, hoping you might review the circumstances under which this non-payment occurred and consider removing the negative trade line from my credit reports.

As soon as I became aware of the balance I contacted ----------------- and paid the balance in full. I provide this not to justify why the account was unpaid, but rather to show that the issue with ----------- is not a good indicator of my actual credit worthiness. I hope that --------is willing to work with me on erasing this mark from my credit reports.

I would like to STRESS that the information currently being reported IS accurate, (I am not disputing anything with ---------------). I am simply asking -------------for a courtesy gesture of goodwill in having the credit bureaus remove this account from my report. I do recognize that this request is unique and that it may not be ------------- normal policy. Please consider that the Fair Credit Reporting Act does not demand that all accounts be reported, only that any account that is reported be reported accurately. Therefore, a company does have legal discretion and permission to remove any account it chooses from the credit report. I'm hoping that ------------- will do that in my case for this account.

Your kind consideration in this matter is greatly appreciated.

Best Regards
Signature
Printed Name

LETTER TO HARASSING CREDITOR

Sally B. Struggle
123 Your College Address
Your College Town, ST 01234

Harassing Creditor
Creditor Address
Anytown, ST 56789

RE: Account Number

Date

Dear Harassing Creditor,

To whom it may concern:

Please be advised that on the following dates, __________________, I requested that your representative __________________ stop calling me at home or at work. These continuous calls are serving no purpose but to harass me. I realize that I have a financial obligation to your company. However, my present financial situation makes it impossible for me to meet our original terms. I am exercising my right granted by the Bureau of Consumer Protection, a division of the Federal
Trade Commission, to request that no one from your company call me at home or at work again.

If you must contact me, please do it via U.S. Postal Service.

Thank you in advance for your cooperation.

Sincerely,
Signature
Printed Name

APPENDIX C
ASSORTED WORKSHEETS

CREATING A PERSONAL FINANCIAL PLAN

These questions are the foundation for creating a personal financial plan.

1. Assessment: *Where are you now*? Use numbers and dollar amounts to be specific about where you are with respect to savings, debt and any other financial data you want to start tracking.

____

____

____

____

____

2. Goal Setting: *Where do you want to be?* Again use specific terms to define where you would like to be financially by a set time at some point in the near future.

____

____

____

3. Creating a Plan: *How will you get there?* Do you need to stop spending or get a job in order to reach your goals? List three things you can begin doing within the next 30 days to get you on track.

4. Execution: *Taking action and making it happen.* There's no time like the present to take action on creating the life you say you want! List an action you can start in the next 24 hours.

5. Re-Assessment: *Repeating the process regularly.* Determine in advance how often throughout the year you will check in on your progress and re-assess if necessary. I would suggest at least every six months.

BUDGETING FOR THE COLLEGE STUDENT

Of course your expenses and therefore, budget, will vary based upon what school you attend, as well as your personal lifestyle habits and even your proximity to home, but this is a great place to begin to list the numbers you'll need to work with. Incorporate this budgeting process into your routine each semester, including summers.

Add up the amount you expect to receive this semester from the following sources. When complete, remember to divide that total by the number of months in the semester, so you can create a monthly budget.

Now, it's time to subtract your monthly fixed expenses from your monthly income. This will tell you exactly how much you can spare on the variable expenses you'll fill in on the next page.

Source of Income	**Semester Total**	**Monthly Budget**
Scholarships and Grants		
Student Loans		
Work Study or Part-Time Work		
Parental Support		
Miscellaneous Source		
Total Income		

Fixed Expenses	**Monthly Cost**	**Semester Total**
Rent		
Estimated Utilities		
Car Payment and/or Insurance		
Cell Phone		
Savings (I don't care if its $5!)		
Other		
Total Fixed Expenses		

Now, it's time to subtract your monthly fixed expenses from your monthly income. This will tell you exactly how much you can spare on the variable expenses you'll fill in on the next page.

Monthly Income $________________
(minus) Fixed Expenses $________________
(equals) Variable Expenses $________________

Variable Expenses	**Monthly Cost**	**Semester Total**
Groceries (Beyond Meal Plan)		
Entertainment & Dining Out		
Laundry		
Gas & Car Maintenance		
Organization or Club Dues		
Other		
Total Variable Expenses		

Once you've completed the entire exercise, you should find that your fixed + variable expenses are LESS THAN or EQUAL to your income. If not, you have to begin making hard decisions about what has to go OR how you will earn additional income for the semester.

CREATING INCOME IN COLLEGE

Answer these questions to help you create a plan for earning additional income in college.

1. Assessment: *What are three things you absolutely enjoy doing*? Be specific about the activities, as well as who you like to do them with or for.

____

____

____

____

____

2. Research: *Is there a need for this service on or around your campus*? Ask friends, staff or even faculty. Google what you are offering and input your zip code. What are people charging? What could you charge? Brainstorm how you can make the service unique, but don't over-analyze. McDonald's never stopped Wendy's or Burger King from being successful in their own right.

____

____

____

____

____

3. Create a Marketing Plan: *How will you get the word out?* Is there a school newspaper? Can you place signs on campus announcement board? Word of mouth? Social media?

____

____

____

____

____

4. Execution: *When will you jump into action.* There's no time like the present. Plan, but only to a point. A plan with faults is better than a perfect plan that no one knows about.

____

____

____

____

____

5. Re-Assessment: *Repeating the process regularly.* If you can earn an extra $100 from your service, you're on to something. Revisit the plan to figure out how you can earn an addition $500 next semester.

____

____

____

____

____

MEET PATRICE C. WASHINGTON

Patrice C. Washington has been making money educational yet fun since 2003. She is a featured columnist, television commentator, author, speaker and leading authority on personal finance, entrepreneurship and success for women and youth.

Patrice's wisdom on money matters has been featured in:

NBC
The Huffington Post
Upscale Magazine
HelloBeautiful.com
Sheen Magazine
BlackEnterprise.com

Each year, universities and colleges nationally have trusted Patrice to entertain, empower and educate thousands of students on their campuses. Why? First of all, she's funny. No, she's really funny. Her humorous stories have a way of drawing audiences in almost immediately and allowing them to look at everyday scenarios in a completely different light. Second, Patrice is transparent. She selflessly tells the story of her own journey and unlike many is not ashamed to share both her triumphs and her setbacks. She enlightens students on why she doesn't run from failure and why they shouldn't either. "It's just a time in my life that didn't go as planned. Now, I have feedback." Lastly, Patrice's brain is jam-packed with practical tips students can take and implement immediately. She doesn't worry people with stiff, financial jargon. She keeps it simple and most importantly, she keeps it real.

When Patrice isn't making audiences laugh and learn somewhere around the country, she's at home in Atlanta, GA being entertained by her highly imaginative little gymnast, Reagan and her secretly hilarious husband, Gerald.

CPSIA information can be obtained at www.ICGtesting.com
Printed in the USA
LVOW08s2249291215

468355LV00014B/480/P